Contents

Introduction

Once after a poetry reading by the late James Simmons I went up to talk to him and bring greetings from a friend. He asked me my name and when I told him said, 'Ah! The anthologist!' My first reaction was to reply, 'I've written other things as well!' but it occurred to me that it was a title not without honour, one that might by approved by the Académie Française. A quick glance at my bookshelf revealed that I had compiled fifteen collections of what General Earl Wavell called 'Other Man's Flowers'. These include *The Derry Anthology, The Homes of Donegal, The Best from The Bell*, an Irish-American collection called *A Little Bit of Heaven*, an anthology of Irish poems called *Taisce Duan* with Jo O'Donoghue and *Rich and Rare*.

The last named was one of the earliest and was assembled because I needed it for my own purposes, professional and private. The poems in it I already knew – or thought I did. But there were extra verses I was not aware of and lines that I had not got precisely right. I needed a collection, handily enclosed in one volume, that would encompass our distressful country for all its chequered history. The word 'heritage' has been badly abused lately but it is the only word that describes the source of so much that has formed us – of whatever persuasion. The contents of *Rich and Rare* were patriotic, sad, funny, romantic, cynical – an assembly kit to build a working Irish person.

Anthologies of any sort need no defence: each of us has built his own mental collection. We are all walking compilations but while the average roomful of Irish people will have a large intersection set of personal choices the pieces not held in common are worth examining and perhaps of incorporation in our own stores. In this sense the Irish word *stór* has a useful double sense: not only a depot where things are made available but a treasure – a kind of moral safety-deposit box where what is nationally precious to us can be kept secure. When MacMorris, the Irish captain in Shakespeare's *Henry V,* asks, 'What ish my nation?' his answer could very well have been some such *stór* as this anthology. The earliest example of such a compilation in modern times was *The Golden Treasury of Best Songs and Lyrical Poems,* compiled by Sir Francis Turner Palgrave (1824–97) in 1861, and that is precisely the connotation of this *stór*.

The Smile and the Tear, like *Rich and Rare,* has a title, slightly emended, from Thomas Moore, one of our neglected treasures. It is a collection for the mythical Irish Everyperson, a travelling companion of things bright and green and elsewhere of more sombre hue but guaranteed Irish throughout. The title is a reminder that, although as a nation we tend to be exuberant, sorrow has also young days shaded.

The various categories have been chosen for convenient accessibility: not only are they not exclusive but they will not contain the favourite poems of many readers. There is no book big enough to satisfy that need and the accusation of perverse inclusion or equally perverse omission is one any compiler has to face. The section titles are quotations from inside each part and are fairly self-explanatory: 'Who Fears to Speak?' deals with aspects of all our histories; 'An Emerald Set in the Ring of the Sea' with what still may be called the 'quiet land of Ireland'; 'Off to Philadelphia' is a true mixture of smile and tear: sorrow at leaving; hope for a better life. 'Four Ducks on a Pond' is about the childhood that passes too soon and the web- or four-footed friends that are often part of it and 'Let us Be Merry!' a reminder that as a nation we can do the smile as well as the next braggart. 'The Gap of Dreams' touches on the spiritual and the mysterious and we do that class of thing pretty well too! 'I Know My Love' seems self-explanatory and we finish with 'All the Sweet Buttermilk', a scenic and topographical tour of the finest holiday location in Europe, weather permitting! Finally 'Cruacha Glas' na hÉireann' is part of another store, a taisce that is an unsloughable part of our past and present persistent psyches.

Who Fears to Speak?

Lilliburlero

Thomas Wharton (1648–1714)

The refrain is a mock version of the Catholic watch cry during the rising of 1641. It is a phonic approximation of An lile ba léir é, ba linne an lá *(The lily prevailed; the day was ours.)*

Ho, brother Teague, dost hear de decree,
Lilliburlero, bullen a la,
Dat we shall have a new deputy?
Lilliburlero, bullen a la.

Chorus
Lero, lero, lilliburlero,
Lilliburlero, bullen a la.
Lero, lero, lilliburlero,
Lilliburlero, bullen a la.

Ho, by my shoul, it is de Talbot,
Lilliburlero, bullen a la,
And he will cut all de English throat.
Lilliburlero, bullen a la.

Though, by my shoul, de English do prate,
Lilliburlero, bullen a la,
De law's on their side and Creish knows what.
Lillilburlero, bullen a la.

But if dispense do come from de Pope,
Lilliburlero, bullen a la,
We'll hang Magna Carta and dem in a rope.
Lilliburlero, bullen a la.

And de good Talbot is made a Lord,
Lilliburlero, bullen a la,
And he with brave lads is coming abroad.
Lilliburlero, bullen a la.

Who in all France have taken a swear,
Lilliburlero, bullen a la,
Dat they will have no Protestant heir.
Lilliburlero, bullen a la.

O, but why does he stay behind?
Lilliburlero, bullen a la,
Ho, by my shoul, 'tis a Protestant wind!
Lilliburlero, bullen a la.

Now Tyrconnel is come ashore,
Lilliburlero, bullen a la,
And we shall have commissions galore.
Lilliburlero, bullen a la.

And he dat will not go to Mass,
Lilliburlero, bullen a la,
Shall turn out and look like an ass.
Lilliburlero, bullen a la.

Now, now de heretics all go down,
Lilliburlero, bullen a la,
By Creish and St. Patrick, de nation's our own.
Lilliburlero, bullen a la.

Dere was an old prophesy found in a bog,
Lilliburlero, bullen a la,
Dat Ireland should be rul'd by an ass and a dog.
Lilliburlero, bullen a la.

Dat prophesy's true and now come to pass,
Lilliburlero, bullen a la,
For Talbot's de dog and Tyrconnel's de ass.
Lilliburlero, bullen a la.

The Wake of William Orr

William Drennan (1754–1820)

William Orr (1766–97) was a United Irishman hanged for administering 'a treasonable oath'.

There our murdered brother lies;
Wake him not with woman's cries;
Mourn the way that manhood ought –
Sit in silent trance of thought.

Write his merits on your mind;
Morals pure and manners kind;
In his head, as on a hill,
Virtue placed her citadel.

Why cut off in palmy youth?
Truth he spoke and acted truth.
'Countrymen, unite,' he cried
And die for what our Saviour died.

God of peace and God of love!
Let it not Thy vengeance move –
Let it not Thy lightning draw –
A nation guillotined by law.

Hapless Nation, rent and torn,
Thou were early taught to mourn;
Warfare for six hundred years!
Epoch marked with blood and tears!

Hunted thro' thy native grounds
Or flung reward to human hounds,
Each one pulled and tore his share,
Heedless of thy deep despair.

Hapless nation, hapless land!
Heap of uncementing sand!

Crumpled by a foreign weight:
And by worse, domestic hate.

God of mercy! God of peace!
Make this mad confusion cease;
O'er the mental chaos move,
Through it speak the light of love.

Monstrous and unhappy sight!
Brothers' blood will not unite;
Holy oil and holy water
Mix and fill the world with slaughter.

Who is she with aspect wild?
The widowed mother with her child –
Child new stirring in the womb
Husband waiting for the tomb!

Angel of this sacred place,
Calm her soul and whisper peace –
Cord or axe or guillotine,
Make the sentence – not the sin.

Here we watch our brother's sleep:
Watch with us but do not weep:
Watch with us thro' dead of night –
But expect the morning light.

Oliver's Advice

William Blacker (1777–1855)

*A poem written in protest at the banning of Orange Order marches in
1850; Oliver is Cromwell and Roden the local landowner who encouraged
the confrontation at Dolly's Brae in 1848 that led to the death of many
Catholics.*

The night is gathering gloomily, the day is closing fast –
The tempest flaps his raven wings in loud and angry blast;
The thunder clouds are driving athwart the lurid sky –
But put your trust in God, my boys, and keep your powder dry.

There was a day when loyalty was hailed with honour due,
Our banner the protection waved to all the good and true –
And gallant hearts beneath its folds were linked in honour's tie,
We put our trust in God, my boys, and kept our powder dry.

When treason bared her bloody arm and maddened round the
    land,
For king and laws and order fair, we drew the ready brand;
Our gathering spell was William's name – our word was, 'Do or die.'
And still we put our trust in God and kept our powder dry.

But now, alas! a wondrous change has come the nation o'er,
And worth and gallant services remembered are no more;
And, crushed beneath oppression's weight, in chains of grief we lie –
But put your trust in God, my boys, and keep your powder dry.

Forth starts the spawn of Treason, the 'scaped of Ninety-eight,
To bask in courtly favour and seize the helm of state –
E'en they whose hands are reeking yet with murder's crimson dye;
But put your trust in God, my boys, and keep your powder dry.

They come, whose deeds incarnadined the Slaney's silver wave –
They come, who to the foreign foe the hail of welcome gave;
He comes, the open rebel fierce – he comes the Jesuit sly;
But put your trust in God, my boys, and keep your powder dry.

They come, whose counsels wrapped the land in foul rebellious flame,
Their hearts unchastened by remorse, their cheeks untinged by shame.
Be still, be still, indignant heart – be tearless, too, each eye –
And put your trust in God, my boys, and keep your powder dry.

The Power that led his chosen, by pillared cloud and flame,
Through parted sea and desert waste, that Power is still the same;
He fails not – He, the loyal hearts that firm on him rely –
So put your trust in God, my boys, and keep your powder dry.

The Power that nerved the stalwart arms of Gideon's chosen few,
The Power that led great William, Boyne's reddening torrent through,
In his protecting aid confide and every foe defy –
Then put your trust in God, my boys, and keep your powder dry.

Already see the star of hope emits its orient blaze,
The cheering beacon of relief it glimmers thro' the haze.
It tells of better days to come, it tells of succour nigh –
Then put your trust in God, my boys, and keep your powder dry.

See, see along the hills of Down its rising glories spread,
But brightest beams its radiance from Donard's lofty head.
Clanbrassil's vales are kindling wide and 'Roden' is the cry –
Then put your trust in God, my boys, and keep your powder dry.

Then cheer, ye hearts of loyalty, nor sink in stark despair,
Our banner shall again unfold its glories to the air.
The storm that raves the wildest the soonest passes by;
Then put your trust in God, my boys, and keep your powder dry.

For 'happy homes', for 'altars free', we grasp the ready sword –
For freedom, truth, and for our God's unmutilated word.
These, these the war-cry of our march, our hope the Lord on high;
Then put your trust in God, my boys, and keep your powder dry.

Oh! Breathe Not His Name

Thomas Moore (1779–1852)

The name is that of the revolutionary, Robert Emmet (1778–1803)

Oh! breathe not his name, let it sleep in the shade
Where, cold and unhonoured, his relics were laid:
Sad, silent and dark, be the tears that we shed,
As the night-dew that falls on the grass o'er his head.

But the night-dew that falls, though in silence it weeps,
Shall brighten with verdure the grave where he sleeps;
And the tear that we shed, though in secret it rolls,
Shall long keep his memory green in our souls.

She Is Far from the Land

Thomas Moore (1779–1852)

'She' is Sarah Curran (1782–1808), Emmet's sweetheart

She is far from the land where her young hero sleeps
And lovers around her are sighing!
But coldly she turns from their gaze, and weeps,
For her heart in his grave is lying!

She sings the wild songs of her dear native plains,
Every note which he loved awaking;
Ah, little they think who delight in her strains,
How the heart of the minstrel is breaking!

He had lived for his love, for his country he died,
They were all that to life had entwined him;
Nor soon shall the tears of his country be dried,
Nor long will his love stay behind him.

Oh! make her a grave, where the sunbeams rest,
When they promise a glorious morrow;
They'll shine o'er her sleep, like a smile from the west,
From her own lov'd island of sorrow!

The Maiden City

Charlotte Elizabeth Tonna (1790–1846)

*Derry is the 'maiden city' because it survived the Siege of 1688-9 and was
never taken. Until the Great Famine of 1845-7 it remained a loyalist city.*

Where Foyle his swelling waters
Rolls northward to the main,
Here, Queen of Erin's daughters,
Fair Derry fixed her reign;
A holy temple crowned her
And commerce graced her street;
A rampart wall was round her,
The river at her feet;
And here she sat alone, boys,
And looking from the hill,
Vowed the Maiden on her throne, boys,
Would be a Maiden still.

From Antrim crossing over
In famous eighty-eight,
A plumed and belted lover
Came to the Ferry Gate.
She summoned to defend her
Our sires – a beardless race –
They shouted 'No Surrender!'
And slammed it in his face.
Then in a quiet tone, boys,
They told him 'twas their will
That the Maiden on her throne, boys,
Should be a Maiden still.

Next crushing all before him
A kingly wooer came
(The royal banner o'er him
Blushed crimson deep for shame);
He showed the Pope's commission,
Nor dreamed to be refused.
She pitied his condition,

But begged to stand excused.
In short, the fact is known, boys,
She chased him from the hill,
For the Maiden on the throne, boys,
Would be a Maiden still.

On our brave sires descending,
'Twas then the tempest broke,
Their peaceful dwellings rending,
'Mid blood and flame and smoke.
That hallowed graveyard yonder
Swells with the slaughtered dead –
O brothers! pause and ponder –
It was for us they bled;
And while their gifts we own, boys –
The fane that tops our hill –
Oh! the Maiden on her throne, boys,
Shall be a Maiden still!

Nor wily tongue shall move us,
Nor tyrant arm affright;
We'll look to One above us
Who ne'er forsook the right;
Who will, may crouch and tender
The birthright of the free
But, brothers, 'No Surrender,'
No compromise for me!
We want no barrier stone, boys,
No gates to guard the hill,
Yet the Maiden on her throne, boys,
Shall be a Maiden still.

from Dark Rosaleen

from the Irish
James Clarence Mangan (1804–49)

Róisín Dubh (Dark Rosaleen) is a personification of the 'most distressful country'.

O, my Dark Rosaleen,
Do not sigh, do not weep!
The priests are on the ocean green;
They march along the deep.
There's wine from the royal Pope,
Upon the ocean green;
And Spanish wine shall give you hope,
My Dark Rosaleen!
     My own Rosaleen!
Shall glad your heart, shall give you hope,
Shall give you health and help and hope,
My Dark Rosaleen!

Over hills and through dales,
Have I roamed for your sake;
All yesterday I sailed with sails
On river and on lake.
The Erne, at its highest flood,
I dashed across unseen,
For there was lightning in my blood,
My Dark Rosaleen!
     My own Rosaleen!
O! there was lightning in my blood;
Red lightning lightened through my blood,
My Dark Rosaleen!

All day long, in unrest,
To and fro, do I move.
The very soul within my breast
Is wasted for you, love!
The heart in my bosom faints
To think of you, my Queen,

My life of life, my saint of saints,
My Dark Rosaleen!
    My own Rosaleen!
To hear your sweet and sad complaints,
My life, my love, my saint of saints
My Dark Rosaleen!

Woe and pain, pain and woe,
Are my lot night and noon,
To see your bright face clouded so,
Like to the mournful moon.
But yet will I rear your throne,
Again in golden sheen;
'Tis you shall reign, shall reign alone,
My Dark Rosaleen!
    My own Rosaleen!
'Tis you shall have the golden throne
My life of life, my saint of saints,
My Dark Rosaleen!

O! the Erne shall run red
With redundance of blood,
The earth shall rock beneath our tread,
And flames wrap hill and wood,
Ere you shall fade, ere you shall die,
My Dark Rosaleen!
    My own Rosaleen!
The judgment hour must first be nigh,
Ere you can fade, ere you can die,
My Dark Rosaleen!

Lament for the Death
of Eoghan Ruadh O'Neill

Thomas Davis (1814–45)

Eoghan Ruadh O'Neill (c. 1582–1649), Irish leader in the Confederate Wars of the 1640s, died, it was believed by poisoning, on 6 November 1649.

'Did they dare, did they dare, to slay Eoghan Ruadh O'Neill?'
'Yes, they slew with poison him they feared to meet with steel.'
'May God wither up their hearts! May their blood cease to flow!
May they walk in living death, who poisoned Eoghan Ruadh!'

'Though it break my heart to hear, say again the bitter words.'
'From Derry, against Cromwell, he marched to measure swords;
But the weapon of the Saxon met him on the way,
And he died at Cloch Uachtar, upon Saint Leonard's day.'

'Wail, wail ye for the Mighty One! Wail, wail ye for the Dead;
Quench the hearth and hold the breath – with ashes strew the head.
How tenderly we loved him! How deeply we deplore!
Holy Saviour! But to think we shall never see him more!

'Sagest in the council was he, kindest in the Hall:
Sure we never won a battle – 'twas Eoghan won them all.
Had he lived – had he lived – our dear country had been free;
But he's dead, but he's dead, and 'tis slaves we'll ever be.

'O'Farrell and Clanricarde, Preston and Red Hugh,
Audley and MacMahon – ye are valiant, wise and true;
But – what, what are ye all to our darling who is gone?
The rudder of our ship was he, our castle's corner-stone!

'Wail, wail him through the island! Weep, weep for our pride!
Would that on the battlefield our gallant chief had died!
Weep the victor of Benburb – weep him, young man and old.
Weep for him, ye women – your beautiful lies cold.

'We thought you would not die – we were sure you would not go,
And leave us in our utmost need to Cromwell's cruel blow –
Sheep without a shepherd, when the snow shuts out the sky –
Oh! why did you leave us, Eoghan! Why did you die?

'Soft as woman's was your voice, O'Neill, bright was your eye
Oh, why did you leave us, Eoghan? Why did you die?
You troubles are all over, you're at rest with God on high;
But we're slaves, and we're orphans, Eoghan! Why did you die?'

Clare's Dragoons

Thomas Davis (1814-45)

A regiment of cavalry raised by Daniel O'Brien of Carrigaholt, 3rd Lord Clare, that served in Ireland on the side of James II but gained far greater distinction fighting for the French in battles like Ramillies (1706) and Fontenoy (1745).

When, on Ramillies' bloody field,
The baffled French were forced to yield,
The victor Saxon backward reeled
Before the charge of Clare's dragoons.
The flags we conquered in that fray,
Look lone in Ypres' choir, they say,
We'll win them company today,
Or bravely die like Clare's dragoons.

Chorus
Viva la, for Ireland's wrong!
Viva la, for Ireland's right!
Viva la, in battle throng,
For a Spanish steed and sabre bright!

The brave old lord died near the fight,
But for each drop he lost that night,
A Saxon cavalier shall bite
The dust before Lord Clare's Dragoons.
For never, when our spurs were set,
And never, when our sabres met,
Could we the Saxon soldiers get
To stand the shock of Clare's dragoons.

Another Clare is here to lead,
The worthy son of such a breed,
The French expect some famous deed,
When Clare leads on his bold dragoons.
Our colonel comes from Brian's race,
His wounds are in his breast and face,

The *bearna baoghail* is still his place,
The foremost of his bold dragoons,

Chorus
Viva la, the new brigade!
Viva la, the old one too!
Viva la, the rose shall fade
And the shamrock shine forever new!

Oh! comrades, think how Ireland pines,
Her exiled lords, her rifled shrines,
Her dearest hope, the ordered lines,
And bursting charge of Clare's dragoons.
Then fling your green flag to the sky,
Be 'Limerick!' your battle-cry,
And charge, till blood flows fetlock-high,
Around the track of Clare's dragoons.

Tone's Grave

Thomas Davis (1814–45)

Wolfe Tone (1763–98) was a founder of the United Irishmen. Bodenstown,
County Kildare, is still a site of Republican pilgrimage.

In Bodenstown Churchyard there is a green grave,
And wildly along it the winter winds rave;
Small shelter, I ween, are the ruined walls there,
When the storm sweeps down on the plains of Kildare.

Once I lay on that sod – it lies over Wolfe Tone –
And I thought how he perished in prison alone,
His friends unavenged and his country unfreed –
'Oh, bitter,' I said, 'is the patriot's meed.

'For in him the heart of a woman combined,
With a heroic life and a governing mind –
A martyr for Ireland – his grave has no stone –
His name seldom named and his virtues unknown.'

I was woke from my dream by the voices and tread,
Of a band, who came into the home of the dead.
They carried no corpse and they carried no stone,
And they stopped when the came to the grave of Wolfe Tone.

There were students and peasants, the wise and the brave,
And an old man who knew him from cradle to grave,
And children who thought me hard-hearted, for they,
On the sanctified ground were forbidden to play.

But the old man who saw I was mourning there, said:
'We come, sir, to weep where young Wolfe Tone is laid,
And we're going to raise him a monument too –
A plain one, yet fit for the simple and true.'

My heart overflowed and I clasped his old hand,
And I blessed him and every one of his band;

'Sweet! sweet! 'tis to find that such faith can remain,
To the cause and the man so long vanquished and slain.'

In Bodenstown Churchyard there is a green grave
And freely around it let winter winds rave –
Far better they suit him – the ruin and gloom,
Till Ireland, a nation, can build him a tomb.

A Nation Once Again

Thomas Davis (1814–45)

In line four the 'three hundred men' are the Spartans, who saved Greece at Thermopylae in 480BC and the 'three men' are Horatius, Herminius and Lartius who in the Roman legend held the bridge against the Etruscan armies of Lars Porsena and saved the city.

When boyhood's fire was in my blood,
I read of ancient freemen.
For Greece and Rome who bravely stood –
Three hundred men and three men.
And then I prayed I yet might see,
Our fetters rent in twain,
And Ireland, long a province, be,
A nation once again.

And from that time, through wildest woe,
That hope has shone, a far light,
Nor could love's brightest summer glow,
Outshine that solemn starlight:
It seemed to watch above my head,
In forum, field and fane;
Its angel voice sang round my bed,
'A nation once again.'

It whispered, too, that freedom's ark,
And service high and holy,
Would be profaned by feelings dark,
And passions vain and lowly:
For freedom comes from God's left hand,
And needs a godly train;
And righteous men must make our land,
A nation once again.

And I as grew from boy to man,
I bent me to that bidding –
My spirit of each selfish plan,
And cruel passion ridding;

For thus I hoped some day to aid –
Oh, can such hope be vain? –
When my dear country shall be made,
A nation once again.

The West's Asleep

Thomas Davis (1814–45)

When all besides a vigil keep,
The west's asleep, the west's asleep –
Alas! and well may Erin weep,
When Connacht lies in slumber deep.
There lakes and plain smile fair and free,
'Mid rocks – their guardian chivalry –
Sing oh! let man learn liberty,
From crashing wind and lashing sea.

That chainless wave and lovely land,
Freedom and nationhood demand –
Be sure, the great God never planned,
For slumbering slaves a land so grand,
And long, a brave and haughty race,
Honoured and sentinelled the place –
Sing oh! not even their son's disgrace,
Can quite destroy their glory's trace.

For often, in O'Connor's van,
To triumph dashed each Connacht clan –
And fleet as deer the Normans ran
Through Corlieu's Pass and Ardrahan.
And other times saw deeds as brave;
And glory guards Clanricard's grave –
Sing oh! they died their land to save,
At Aughrim's slopes and Shannon's wave.

And if, when all a vigil keep,
The west's asleep, the west's asleep –
Alas! and well may Erin weep,
That Connacht lies in slumber deep,
But – hark! –some voice like thunder spake,
'The West's awake, the West's awake –
'Sing oh! hurrah! let England quake,
We'll watch till death for Erin's sake.'

The March to Kinsale

Aubrey de Vere (1814-1902)

Kinsale was the last (unsuccessful) battle of the Nine Years' War (1594-1603). The Ulster chieftains, Hugh O'Neill and Hugh O'Donnell, marched south to join a Spanish force and fight the English in the winter of 1601.

O'er many a river bridged with ice,
Through many a vale with snowdrifts dumb,
Past quaking fen and precipice,
The Princes of the North are come!

Lo, these are they that year by year,
Roll'd back the tide of England's war;
Rejoice, Kinsale! Thy help is near!
That wondrous winter march is o'er.

Blithe as a boy on marched the host,
With droning pipe and clear-voiced harp;
At last above that southern coast
Rang out their war-steeds' whinny sharp.

And up the sea-salt slopes they wound,
And airs once more of ocean quaff'd:
Those frosty woods the rocks that crown'd,
As though May touched them, waved and laugh'd.

And thus they sang, 'Tomorrow morn
Our eyes shall rest upon the foe:
Roll on swift night, in silence borne,
And blow, thou breeze of sunrise, blow!'

The Wearing of the Green

Dion Boucicault (1822–90)

Napper Tandy (1740–1803) was a United Irishman.

O Paddy dear, and did you hear the news that's going round?
The shamrock is forbid by law to grow on Irish ground.
St Patrick's Day no more we'll keep, his colours can't be seen,
For there's a cruel law again the wearing of the green.
I met with Napper Tandy and he took me by the hand,
And said, 'How's poor old Ireland and how does she stand?'
She's the most distressful country that ever yet was seen.
They're hanging men and women for the wearing of the Green.

Then since the colour we must wear is England's cruel red,
Sure Ireland's sons will ne'er forget the blood that they have shed.
You may take the shamrock from your hat and cast it on the sod,
But 'twill take root and flourish though underfoot 'tis trod.
When law can stop the blades of grass from growing as they grow,
And when the leaves in summertime their verdure dare not show,
Then I will change the colour that I wear in my caubeen,
But till that day, please God, I'll stick to wearing of the Green.

But if at last our colour should be torn from Ireland's heart,
Her sons with shame and sorrow from the dear old isle will part.
I've heard a whisper of a country that lies beyond the sea,
Where rich and poor stand equal in the light of freedom's day.
O Erin, must we leave you, driven by a tyrant's hand?
Must we ask a mother's blessing from a strange and distant land?
Where the cruel cross of England shall never more be seen,
And where, please God, we'll live and die still wearing of the Green.

The Memory of the Dead

John Kells Ingram (1823–1907)

Who fears to speak of Ninety-eight?
Who blushes at the name?
When cowards mock the patriot's fate,
Who hangs his head for shame?
He's all a knave or half a slave,
Who slights his country thus;
But a true man, like you, man,
Will fill your glass with us.

We drink the memory of the brave,
The faithful and the few;
Some lie afar beyond the wave,
Some sleep in Ireland, too;
All, all are gone; but still lives on,
The fame of those who died;
All true men, like you, men,
Remember them with pride.

Some on the shores of distant lands
Their weary hearts have laid,
And by the stranger's heedless hands,
Their lonely graves were made;
But though their clay be far away,
Beyond the Atlantic foam,
In true men, like you, men,
Their spirit's still at home.

The dust of some is Irish earth,
Among their own they rest,
And the same land that gave them birth,
Has caught them to her breath;
And we will pray that from their clay,
Full many a race may start,
Of true men, like you, men,
To act as brave a part.

They rose in dark and evil days,
To right their native land;
They kindled here a living blaze,
That nothing shall withstand.
Alas! that might can vanquish right –
They fell and passed away;
But true men, like you, men,
Are plenty here today.

Then here's their memory – may it be
For us a guiding light,
To cheer our strife for liberty,
And each us to unite –
Through good and ill, be Ireland's still,
Though sad as theirs your fate,
And true men, be you, men,
Like those of Ninety-eight.

O'Donnell Abú

Michael Joseph McCann (1824–83)

Saimear is near Ballyshannon, County Donegal.

Proudly the note of the trumpet is sounding,
Loudly the war-cries arise on the gale;
Fleetly the steed by Lough Swilly is bounding,
To join the thick squadrons in Saimear's green vale.
On, ev'ry mountaineer,
Strangers to flight and fear!
Rush to the standards of dauntless Red Hugh!
Bonnaught and gallowglass,
Throng from each mountain pass;
On for old Erin, 'O'Donnell Abú!'

Princely O'Neill to our aid is advancing,
With many a chieftain and warrior clan,
A thousand proud steeds in his vanguard are prancing,
'Neath the borderers brave from the banks of the Bann;
Many a heart shall quail,
Under its coat of mail;
Deeply the merciless foeman shall rue,
When on his ear shall ring,
Borne on the breezes' wing
Tir Connell's dread war-cry, 'O'Donnell Abú!

Wildly o'er Desmond the war-wolf is howling,
Fearless the eagle sweeps over the plain,
The fox in the streets of the city is prowling;
All, all who would scare them are banished or slain.
Grasp every stalwart hand,
Hackbut and battle brand,
Pay them all back the debt so long due;
Norris and Clifford well,
Can of Tir Connell tell;
Onward to glory, 'O'Donnell Abú!'

Sacred the cause of Clan Conaill's defending,
The altars we kneel at, the homes of our sires;
Ruthless the ruin the foe is extending,
Midnight is red with the plunderers' fires.
On with O'Donnell, then,
Fight the old fight again,
Sons of Tir Connell, all valiant and true.
Make the false Saxon feel,
Erin's avenging steel!
Strike for your country. 'O Donnell Abú!'

God Save Ireland

Timothy Daniel Sullivan (1827-1914)

Written to commemorate the three Fenians – Michael Larkin, William Phillip Allen and Michael O'Brien – who were executed in Manchester in 1867 and known as the 'Manchester Martyrs'.

High upon the gallows tree swung the noble-hearted three,
By the vengeful tyrant stricken in their bloom;
But they met him face to face, with the courage of their race,
And they went with souls undaunted to their doom.

Chorus
'God save Ireland!' said the heroes;
'God save Ireland!' said they all.
Whether on the scaffold high,
Or the battlefield we die,
Oh, what matter when for Erin dear we fall!

Girt around with cruel foes, still their courage proudly rose,
For they thought of hearts that loved them far and near;
Of the millions true and brave o'er the ocean's swelling wave,
And the friends in holy Ireland ever dear.

Climbed they up the rugged stair, rang their voices out in prayer,
Then with England's fatal cord around them cast,
Close beside the gallows tree kissed like brothers lovingly,
True to home and faith and freedom to the last.

Never till the latest day shall the memory pass away,
Of the gallant lives thus given for our land;
But on the cause must go, amidst joy and weal and woe,
Till we make our isle a nation free and grand.

The Rising of the Moon

John Keegan Casey (1846–70)

'Oh! then tell me, Shawn O'Ferrall,
Tell me why you hurry so?'
'Hush, ma bouchal, hush and listen,'
And his cheeks were all aglow.
'I bear ordhers from the captain,
Get you ready quick and soon,
For the pikes must be together,
At the risin' of the moon.'

'Oh! then tell me, Shawn O'Ferrall,
Where the gatherin' is to be?'
'In the ould spot by the river,
Right well known to you and me.
One word more – for signal token,
Whistle up the martial tune,
With your pike upon your shoulder,
By the risin' of the moon.'

Out from many a mud-wall cabin,
Eyes were watching thro' that night,
Many a manly chest was throbbing,
For the blessed warning light.
Murmurs passed along the valleys,
Like the banshee's lonely croon,
And a thousand blades were flashing,
At the risin' of the moon.'

There beside the singing river,
That dark mass of men was seen,
Far above the shining weapons,
Hung their own beloved green.
'Death to every foe and traitor!
Forward! Strike the marchin' tune,
And hurrah, my boys, for freedom!
'Tis the risin' of the moon.'

Well they fought for poor old Ireland,
And full bitter was their fate.
(Oh! what glorious pride and sorrow,
Fill the name of Ninety-eight.)
Yet, thank God, e'en still are beating,
Hearts in manhood's burning noon,
Who would follow in their footsteps,
At the risin' of the moon.

The Croppy Boy: A Ballad of '98

William McBurney (1844–92)

'Good men and true in this house who dwell,
To a stranger bouchal, I pray you tell,
Is the priest at home or may he be seen?
I would speak a word with Father Green.'

'The priest's at home, boy, and may be seen,
'Tis easy speaking with Father Green;
But you must wait till I go and see,
If the holy father alone may be.'

The youth has entered an empty hall –
What a lonely sound has his light footfall!
And the gloomy chamber's chill and bare,
With a vested priest in a lonely chair.

The youth has knelt to tell his sins.
'Nomine Dei,' the youth begins;
At 'mea culpa' he beats his breast,
And in broken murmurs he speaks the rest.

'At the siege of Ross did my father fall
And at Gorey my loving brothers all.
I alone am left of my name and race.
I will go to Wexford and take their place.

'I cursed three times since last Easter Day.
At Mass-time once I went to play.
I passed the churchyard one day in haste,
And forget to pray for my mother's rest.

'I bear no hate against living thing,
But I love my country above my king.
Now, Father, bless me and let me go,
To die if God has ordained it so.'

The priest said nought but a rustling noise,
Made the youth look up in wild surprise.
The robes were off and in scarlet there,
Sat a yeoman captain with fiery glare.

With fiery glare and fury hoarse,
Instead of a blessing he breathed a curse:
"'Twas a good thought, boy, to come here and shrive,
For one short hour is your time to live.

'Upon yon rivers three tenders float.
The priest's in one, if he isn't shot.
We hold his house for our Lord the King
And, amen, say I, may all traitors swing!'

At Geneva Barracks that young man died,
And at Passage was his body laid.
Good people who live in peace and joy,
Breathe a prayer, shed a tear for the Croppy Boy.

Boolavogue

Patrick Joseph McCall (1861–1919)

Fr John Murphy was tortured, hanged and beheaded after the battle of Vinegar Hill in June 1798.

At Boolavogue, as the sun was setting,
O'er the bright May meadows of Shelmalier,
A rebel hand set the heather blazing,
And brought the neighbours from far and near.
Then Father Murphy, from old Kilcormack,
Spurred up the rock with a warning cry:
'Arm! Arm!' he cried, 'for I've come to lead you;
For Ireland's freedom we fight or die.'

He led us on 'gainst the coming soldiers,
And the cowardly yeomen we put to flight;
'Twas at the Harrow, the boys of Wexford,
Showed Bookey's regiment how men could fight.
Look out for hirelings, King George of England,
Search every kingdom where breathes a slave,
For Father Murphy of County Wexford,
Sweeps o'er the land like a mighty wave.

We took Camolin and Enniscorthy,
And Wexford storming drove out the foes;
'Twas at Slieve Coillte our pikes were reeking,
With the crimson stream of the beaten yeos.
At Tubberneering and Ballyellis,
Full many a Hessian lay in his gore;
Ah, Father Murphy, had aid come over,
The green flag floated from shore to shore.

At Vinegar Hill, o'er the pleasant Slaney,
Our heroes vainly stood back-to-back;
And the yeos at Tullow took Father Murphy
And burned his body upon the rack.

God grant you glory, brave Father Murphy,
And open Heaven to all your men.
The cause that called you may call tomorrow,
In another fight for the green again.

Kelly, the Boy from Killane

Patrick Joseph McCall (1861–1919)

John Kelly was a United Irishman leader from the Shelmalier valley of County Wexford.

What's the news? What's the news, O my bold Shelmalier,
With your long-barrelled gun from the sea?
Say, what wind from the south blows the messenger here,
With a hymn of the dawn for the free?
Goodly news! Goodly news! Do I bring, youth of Forth.
Goodly news shall you hear, Bargy man,
For the boys march at dawn from the south to the north,
Led by Kelly, the Boy from Killane.

Tell me, who is the giant with the gold curling hair,
He who rides at the head of your band?
Seven feet is his height with some inches to spare,
And he looks like a king in command.
Ah! Me lads, that's the pride of the bold Shelmalier,
'Mongst our heroes the bravest of men,
Fling your beavers aloft and give three ringing cheers,
For John Kelly, the Boy from Killane.

Enniscorthy's in flames and old Wexford is won,
And tomorrow the Barrow we'll cross.
On a hill o'er the town they have planted a gun,
That will batter the gateway to Ross.
And the Forth man and Bargy men will march o'er the heath,
With brave Harvey to lead in the van,
But the foremost of all in that grim gap of death,
Will be Kelly, the Boy from Killane.

But the gold sun of freedom grew darkened at Ross,
And it set by the Slaney's red wave,
And poor Wexford stripped naked, hung high on a cross,
With her heart pierced by traitors and slaves.

Glory Oh! Glory Oh! To the brave men who died,
For the cause of long downtrodden man,
Glory Oh! To Mount Leinster's own darlin' and pride,
Dauntless Kelly, the Boy from Killane.

Mise Éire

Pádraic Pearse (1879–1916)

I am Ireland; I am older than the Old Woman of Beare.
Great my joy: I that bore Cúchulainn the valiant.
Great my shame: my own children that sold their mother.
I am lonelier than the Old Woman of Beare.

from The Man from God-Knows-Where

Florence Mary Wilson (d. 1947)

The man was Thomas Russell (1767–1803) a United Irishman.

Into our townlan' on a night of snow,
Rode a man from God-knows-where;
None of us bade him stay or go,
Nor deemed him friend nor damned him foe,
But we stabled his big roan mare:
For in our townlan' we're decent folk,
And if he didn't speak, why none of us spoke,
And we sat till the fire burned low.

We're a civil sort in our wee place,
So we made the circle wide,
Round Andy Lemon's cheerful blaze,
And wished the man his length of days,
And a good end to his ride.
He smiled in under his slouchy hat,
Says he: 'There's a bit of a joke in that,
For we ride different ways.'

The whiles we smoked we watched him stare,
From his seat fornenst the glow.
I nudged Joe Moore: 'You wouldn't dare,
To ask him who he's for meeting there,
And how far he has got to go?'
And Joe wouldn't dare, nor Wully Scott,
And he took no drink – neither cold nor hot,
This man from God-knows-where.

It was closin' time an' late forbye
When us ones braved the air –
I never saw worse (may I live or die)
Than the sleet that night, an' I says, says I:
'You'll find he's for stopping there.'

But at screek o' day, through the gable pane,
I watched him spur in the peltin' rain
And I juked from his rovin' eye.

Two winters more, then the Trouble Year,
When the best a man can feel,
Was the pike he kept in hidin's near,
'Till the blood o' hate and the blood o' fear
Would be redder nor rust on the steel.
Us ones quiet from minding the farms;
Let them take what we gave wi' the weight o' our arms
From Saintfield to Kilkeel.

In the time o' the hurry, we had no lead,
We all of us fought with the rest –
An' if e'er a one shook like a tremblin' reed,
None of us gave neither hint nor heed,
Nor ever even'd we'd guessed.
We men of the North had a word to say,
An' we said it then in our own dour way,
An' we spoke as we thought was best.

...

Well 'twas getting' on past the heat o' the year,
When I rode to Newtown fair:
I sold as I could (the dealers were near –
Only three pounds eight for the Innish steer
An' nothin' at all for the mare!)
I met McKee in the throng o' the street.
Says he: 'The grass has grown under our feet,
Since they hanged young Warwick here.'

And he told me that Boney had promised help,
To a man in Dublin town.
Says he: 'If ye've laid the pike on the shelf,
Ye'd better go home hotfut by yerself,
An' once more take it down.'
So by Comber road I trotted the grey,

49

And never cut corn until Killyleagh,
Stood plain on the rising groun'.

For a wheen o' days we sat waitin' the word,
To rise and go at it like men.
But no French ships sailed into Cloughey Bay,
And we heard the black news on a harvest day:
The cause was lost again;
And Joe and me and Wully Boy Scott,
We agreed to ourselves we'd as lief as not,
Ha' been found in the thick o' the slain.

By Downpatrick gaol I was bound to fare,
On a day I'll remember, feth,
For when I came to the prison square,
The people were waitin' in hundreds here,
And you wouldn't hear stir nor breath!
For the sodgers were standing, grim and tall,
Round a scaffold built there fornenst the wall,
An' a man stepped out for death!

I was brave an' near to the edge of the throng,
Yet I knowed the face again,
An' I knowed the set an' I knowed the walk,
An' the sound of his strange up-country talk,
For he spoke out right an' plain.
Then he bowed his head to the swinging rope,
Whiles I said, 'Please God' to his dying prayer,
That the wrong would cease and the right prevail;
For the man that they hanged at Downpatrick Gaol,
Was the Man from God-knows-where.

The Shan Van Vocht

Anon

An Seanbhean bhocht (Irish: 'the poor old woman') is a personification of Ireland.

'Oh! the French are on the say!'
Says the Shan Van Vocht;
'Oh! the French are on the say!'
Says the Shan Van Vocht.
'Oh! the French are in the bay!'
They'll be here at break of day,
And the Orange will decay,'
Says the Shan Van Vocht,
And the Orange will decay,'
Says the Shan Van Vocht.

'And where will they have their camp?'
Says the Shan Van Vocht.
'And where will they have their camp?'
Says the Shan Van Vocht.
'On the Curragh of Kildare
And the boys will all be there,
With their pikes in good repair,'
Says the Shan Van Vocht,
'With their pikes in good repair,'
Says the Shan Van Vocht.

'And what colour will be seen?'
Says the Shan Van Vocht;
And what colour will be seen?'
Says the Shan Van Vocht.
'What colour should be seen,
Where our fathers' homes have been,
But our own immortal green,'
Says the Shan Van Vocht;
But our own immortal green,'
Says the Shan Van Vocht.

'Will old Ireland then be free?'
Says the Shan Van Vocht;
'Will old Ireland then be free?'
Says the Shan Van Vocht.
'Old Ireland shall be free,
From the centre to the sea, –
Then hurrah for liberty!'
Says the Shan Van Vocht;
'Then hurrah for liberty!'
Says the Shan Van Vocht.

The Ballad of Henry Joy

Anon

Henry Joy McCracken (1767-1798), leader of the United Irish rebellion in Antrim, was executed in Belfast on 17 July 1798.

An Ulsterman I'm proud to be.
From the Antrim glens I come.
Although I labour by the sea,
I have followed flag and drum.
I have heard the martial tramp of men;
I have watched them fight and die,
And it's well do I remember,
When I followed Henry Joy.

I pulled my boat up from the sea;
I hid my sails away;
I hung my nets on a greenwood tree,
And I scanned the moonlit bay.
The boys went out and the Redcoats too;
I kissed my wife goodbye,
And in the shade of the greenwood glade,
Sure I followed Henry Joy.

In Antrim town the tyrant stood.
He tore our ranks with ball.
But with a cheer and a pike to clear,
We swept them o'er the wall.
Our pikes and sabres flashed that day.
We won but lost. Ah, why?
No matter, lads, I fought beside,
And shielded Henry Joy.

We fought for Ireland's glory then;
For home and shire we bled.
Though our numbers few, our hearts beat true,
And five to one lay dead.
But many a lassie mourned her lad,
And mother mourned her boy,

For youth was strong in that gallant throng,
Who followed Henry Joy.

In Belfast town they built a tree,
And the Redcoats mustered there.
I saw him come as the beat of the drum,
Rolled out from the barrack square.
He kissed his sister, went aloft,
Then bade a last goodbye,
And as he died he turned and cried:
'You have murdered Henry Joy.'

John Mitchel's Farewell to His Country

Anon

John Mitchel (1815–75) a Young Irelander, was sentenced to transportation to Bermuda (and then Tasmania) for treason in 1848.

I am a true-born Irishman, John Mitchel is my name;
When I first joined my countrymen from Newry town I came;
I laboured hard both day and night to free my native land,
And for that I was transported unto Van Diemen's Land.

When I first joined my countrymen it was in forty-two,
And what did happen after that I'll quickly tell to you;
I raised the standard of Repeal; I gloried in the deed.
I vowed to Heaven I ne'er would rest till Ireland would be freed.

Farewell, my gallant comrades, it grieves my heart full sore,
To think that I must part from you, perhaps for ever more.
The love I bear my native land, I know no other crime;
That is the reason I must go unto a foreign clime.

As I lay in iron bounds, before my trial day,
My loving wife came to my cell and thus to me did say:
'Cheer up, my gallant husband, undaunted always be;
'Tis better to die a thousand deaths than live in slavery.'

I said, 'My daring girl, it grieves my heart full sore,
To think that I must part from you, perhaps for ever more;
Also my friends and relatives will mourn my sad downfall
But to part from my native land, it grieves me more than all.'

I was quickly placed in the dock, still in strong irons bound,
Whilst numbers of my countrymen were gathered all around;
I was offered then my liberty if I'd deny the cause,
But I'd rather die on a gallows high than suffer tyrant laws.

I was placed on board a convict ship without the least delay.
For Bermuda's Isle our course was steered; I'll ne'er forget the day;

And as I stood upon the deck to take a farewell view,
I shed a tear, but not for fear, my native land for you.

Adieu, Adieu, to sweet Belfast, likewise to Dublin too,
And to my young and tender babes; alas, what will they do?
But one request I ask of you, when your liberty you gain,
Remember Mitchel, far away, a convict o'er the main.

Bold Robert Emmet

Anon

The struggle is over, the boys are defeated,
Old Ireland's surrounded with sadness and gloom,
We were defeated and shamefully treated,
And I, Robert Emmet, awaiting my doom.
Hung, drawn and quartered, sure that was my sentence,
But soon I will show them no coward am I.
My crime is the love of the land I was born in,
A hero I lived and a hero I'll die.

Chorus
Bold Robert Emmet, the darling of Ireland,
Bold Robert Emmet will die with a smile,
Farewell companions, both loyal and daring,
I'll lay down my life for the Emerald Isle.

The barque lay at anchor awaiting to bring me,
Over the billows to the land of the free;
But I must see my sweetheart for I know she will cheer me,
And with her I will sail far over the sea.
But I was arrested and cast into prison,
Tried as a traitor, a rebel, a spy;
But no man can call me a knave or a coward,
A hero I lived and a hero I'll die.

Hark! the bell's tolling, I well know its meaning,
My poor heart tells me it is my death knell;
In come the clergy, the warder is leading,
I have no friends here to bid me farewell.
Goodbye, old Ireland, my parents and sweetheart,
Companions in arms to forget you must try;
I am proud of the honour, it was only my duty
A hero I lived and a hero I'll die.

Old Skibbereen

Anon

The town of Skibbereen in west Cork has become associated in the public imagination with some of the worst suffering of the Great Famine of the 1840s.

'O, father dear, I oft times hear you speak of Erin's Isle,
Her lofty scenes, her valleys green, her mountains rude and wild,
They say it is a lovely land wherein a prince might dwell,
So why did you abandon it, the reason to me tell.'

'My son, I loved my native land with energy and pride,
Till a blight came over all my crops and my sheep and cattle died,
The rents and taxes were to pay and I could not them redeem,
And that's the cruel reason why I left old Skibbereen.

''Tis well I do remember that bleak November day,
When the bailiff and the landlord came to drive us all away,
They set the roof on fire with their cursed English spleen,
And that's another reason why I left old Skibbereen.

'Your mother, too, God rest her soul, lay on the snowy ground,
She fainted in her anguish, seeing the desolation round,
She never rose, but passed away from life to immortal dreams,
And that's another reason why I left old Skibbereen.

'Then sadly I recall the days of gloomy forty-eight,
I rose in vengeance with the boys to battle again' fate,
We were hunted through the mountains as traitors to the queen,
And that, my boy, is the reason why I left old Skibbereen.

'Oh you were only two years old and feeble was your frame,
I could not leave you with my friends for you bore your father's name,
So I wrapped you in my *cóta mór* at the dead of night unseen,
And I heaved a sigh and I said goodbye to dear old Skibbereen.'

'Well, father dear, the day will come when on vengeance we will call,
And Irishmen both stout and tall will rally unto the call,
I'll be the man to lead the van beneath the flag of green,
And loud and high we'll raise the cry, "Revenge for Skibbereen".'

Kevin Barry

Anon

Kevin Barry (1902-1920), the first Republican to be executed since 1916, was hanged on 1 November 1920 for taking part in an ambush on British soldiers in Dublin.

Mountjoy Jail one Monday morning, high above the gallows tree,
Kevin Barry gave his young life for the cause of liberty,
Just a lad of eighteen summers, yet there's no one can deny,
As he marched to death that morning, he proudly held his head on high.

Just before he faced the hangman in his dreary prison cell,
British soldiers tortured Barry because he would not tell,
The names of his brave comrades and other things they wished to know,
'Turn informer or we'll kill you.' Kevin Barry answered, 'No'.

Calmly standing to attention while he bade his last farewell,
To his broken-hearted mother whose sad grief no one can tell,
For the cause he proudly cherished, this sad parting had to be,
Then to death walked softly, smiling, that old Ireland might be free.

Another martyr for old Ireland, another murder for the crown,
Whose brutal laws may kill the Irish, but can't keep their spirits down,
Lads like Barry are no cowards, for the cause they will not lie,
Lads like Barry will free Ireland, for her sake we'll live and die.

An Emerald Set in the Ring of the Sea

Invitation

Anon

I am of Ireland,
And of the holy land
   Of Ireland.
Good sir, pray I thee,
For of Saint Charité,
Come and dance with me,
In Ireland.

Come to the Bower

Anon

Will you come the bower o'er the free boundless ocean
Where the stupendous waves roll in thunderous motion,
Where the mermaids are seen and the fierce tempest gathers
To loved Erin the green, the dear land of our fathers?

Chorus
Will you come, will you, will you, will you come to the bower?

Will you come to the land of O'Neill and O'Donnell,
Of Lord Lucan of old and immortal O'Connell,
Where Brian drove the Danes and St Patrick the vermin
And whose valleys remain still most beautiful and charming.

You can visit Benburb and the storied Blackwater,
Where Owen Roe met Munro and his chieftains did slaughter,
Where lambs skip and play on the mosy all over
From those bright golden views to enchanting Rostrevor.

You can see Dublin city, and the fine groves of Blarney,
The Bann, Boyne and Liffey and the Lakes of Killarney,
You may ride on the tide on the broad majestic Shannon,
You may sail round Loch Neagh and see storied Dungannon.

You can visit New Ross, gallant Wexford and Gorey,
Where the green was last seen by proud Saxon and Tory,
Where the soil is sanctified by the blood of each true man,
Where they died satisfied their enemies they would not run from.

Will you come and awake our lost land from its slumber,
And her fetters we'll break, links that long are encumbered.
And the air will resound with hosannahs to greet you,
On the shore will be found gallant Irishmen to greet you.

Cushla Machree

John Philpot Curran (1750–1817)

Cushla machree (Irish cuisle mo chroí) = 'pulse of my heart'

Dear Erin, how sweetly thy green bosom rises!
An emerald set in the ring of the sea!
Each blade of thy meadows my faithful heart prizes,
Thou queen of the west, the world's cushla machree!

Thy gates open wide to the poor and the stranger –
There smiles hospitality hearty and free;
Thy friendship is seen in the moment of danger,
And the wand'rer is welcomed with cushla machree.

Thy sons they are brave; but, the battle once over,
In brotherly love with their foes they agree,
And the roseate cheeks of thy daughters discover,
The soul-speaking blush that says cushla machree.

Then flourish for ever, my dear native Erin!
While sadly I wander an exile from thee;
And, firm as thy mountains, no injury fearing,
May heaven defend its own cushla machree.

Éire

William Drennan (1754–1820)

When Éire first rose from the dark-swelling flood,
God blessed the green island and saw it was good;
The emerald of Europe, it sparkled and shone,
In the ring of the world the most precious stone.
In her sun, in her soil, in her station thrice blest,
With her back towards Britain, her face to the west,
Éire stands proudly insular on her steep shore,
And strikes her high harp 'mid the ocean's deep roar.

But when its soft tones seem to mourn and to weep,
A dark chain of silence is thrown o'er the deep.
At the thought of the past the tears gush from her eyes,
And the pulse of her heart makes her white bosom rise.
O sons of green Éire, lament o'er the time,
When religion was war and our country a crime.
When man in God's image inverted His plan
And moulded his God in the image of man.

When the interest of state wrought the general woe,
The stranger a friend and the native a foe;
While the mother rejoiced o'er her children oppressed,
And clasped the invader more close to her breast;
When, with Pale for the body and Pale for the soul,
Church and state joined in compact to conquer the whole
And as Shannon was stained with Milesian blood
Eyed each other askance and pronounced it was good.

By the groans that ascend from your forefathers' grave,
For their country thus left to the brute and the slave,
Drive the demon of bigotry home to its den,
And where Britain made brutes now let Éire make men.
Let my sons like the leaves of the shamrock unite,
A partition of sects from one footstalk of right,
Give each his full share of the earth and the sky,
Nor fatten the slave where the serpent would die.

Alas for poor Éire that some are still seen,
Who would dye the grass red from their hatred to green.
Yet, O! when you're up and they're down, let them live;
Then yield them that mercy which they would not give.
Arm of Éire, be strong but be gentle as brave,
And, uplifted to strike, be still ready to save!
Let no feeling of vengeance presume to defile,
The cause of, or men of, the Emerald Isle.

The cause it is good and the men they are true,
And the green shall outlive both the orange and blue!
And the triumph of Éire her daughters shall share,
With the full swelling chest and the fair flowing hair.
Their bosom heaves high for the worthy and brave,
But no coward shall rest on that soft-swelling wave.
Men of Éire, awake and make haste to be blest!
Rise – Arch of the Ocean and Queen of the West!

The Green Little Shamrock of Ireland

Andrew Cherry (1762–1812)

There's a dear little plant that grows in our isle;
'Twas St Patrick himself sure that set it;
And the sun on his labour with pleasure did smile;
And with dew from his eye often wet it.
It thrives through the bog, through the brake and the mire land,
And he called it the dear little shamrock of Ireland.

Chorus
The dear little shamrock, the sweet little shamrock.
The dear little, sweet little, shamrock of Ireland.

This dear little plant still grows in our land.
Fresh and fair as the daughters of Erin,
Whose smiles can bewitch, whose eyes can command,
In each climate that they may appear in.
And shine through the bog, through the brake and the mire land,
Just like their own dear little shamrock of Ireland.

This dear little plant that springs from our soil,
When its three little leaves are extended,
Denotes on one stalk we together should toil;
And ourselves by ourselves be befriended.
And still through the bog, through the brake and the mire land,
From one root should branch, like the shamrock of Ireland.

from The Irishman

James Orr (1770–1816)

The savage loves his native shore,
Though rude the soil and chill the air;
Then well may Erin's sons adore,
Their isle, which Nature formed so fair.
What flood reflects a shore so sweet,
As Shannon great or pastoral Bann?
Or who a friend or foe can meet,
So generous as an Irishman?

His hand is rash, his heart is warm,
But honesty is still his pride;
None more repents a deed of harm,
And none forgives with nobler pride;
He may be duped but won't be dared –
More fit to practise than to plan;
He dearly earns his poor reward,
And spend it like an Irishman.

By honour bound in woe or weal,
Whate'er she bids he dares to do;
Try him with bribes – they won't prevail;
Prove him in fire – you'll find him true.
He seeks not safety, let his post,
Be where it ought, in danger's van;
And if the field of fame be lost,
It won't be by an Irishman.

Erin! Loved land! From age to age,
Be thou more great, more famed and free;
May peace be thine or shouldst thou wage,
Defensive war, cheap victory.
May plenty bloom in very field,
Which gently breezes softly fan;
And cheerful smiles serenely gild,
The home of every Irishman!

Rich and Rare

Thomas Moore (1779–1852)

Rich and rare were the gems she wore,
And a bright gold ring on her wand she bore.
But oh! her beauty was far beyond,
Her sparkling gems or snow-white wand.

'Lady dost thou not fear to stray,
So lone and lovely thro' this bleak way?
Are Erin's sons so good or so cold,
As not to be tempted by woman or gold?'

'Sir Knight, I feel not the least alarm;
No son of Erin shall offer me harm,
For though they love woman and golden store,
Sir Knight, they love honour and virtue more!

On she went and her maiden smile,
In safety lighted her round the Green Isle;
And blest for ever is she who relied,
Upon Erin's honour and Erin's pride.

My Mountain Glens

William Carleton (1794–1869)

Pure was the breeze that fanned my cheek,
As o'er Knockmanny's brow I went;
When every lonely dell could speak,
In airy music vision-sent.
False world, I hate thy cares and thee;
I hate the treacherous haunts of men;
Give back my early life to me;
Give back to me my mountain glen.

How light my youthful visions shone,
When spanned by Fancy's radiant form!
But now the glittering bow is gone,
And leaves me but the cloud and storm.
With wasted form and cheeks all pale,
With heart long seared by grief and pain,
Dunroe, I'll seek my native vale,
And tread my mountain glens again.

from The Exile's Return

John Locke (1847–89)

M'anam do Dhia but there it is –
The dawn on the hills of Ireland!
God's angels lifting the night's black veil,
From the fair, sweet face of my sireland!
O Ireland! isn't it grand you look –
Like a bride in her rich adorning!
With all the pent-up love of my heart,
I bid you the top of the morning.

This one short hour pays lavishly back,
For many a year of mourning;
I'd almost venture another flight,
There's so much joy in returning –
Watching out for the hallowed shore,
All other attractions scorning;
O Ireland! don't you hear me shout?
I bid you the top of the morning.

See how Cliodhna's shelving strand,
The surges are grandly beating;
And Kerry is pushing her headlands out
To give us kindly greeting!
Into the shore the seabirds fly,
On pinions that know no drooping,
And out from the cliffs, with welcome charged,
A million waves come trooping.

O kindly generous Irish land,
So loyal and fair and loving!
No wonder the wandering Celt should think,
And dream of you in his roving.
The alien home may have gems of gold;
Shadows may never have gloomed it;
But the heart will sigh for the absent land,
Where the lovelight first illumed it.

And doesn't old Cobh look charming there,
Watching the wild waves' motion,
Leaning her back up against the hills,
And the tip of her toes in the ocean.
I wonder I don't hear the Shandon bells –
Ah! maybe their chiming's over.
For it's many a year since I began,
The life of a western rover.

For forty summers, a stór mo chroi
Those hills I now feast my eyes on,
Ne'er met my vision save when they rose
Over memory's dim horizon.
E'en so, 'twas grand and fair they seemed,
In the landscape spread before me;
But dreams are dreams and my eyes would ope,
To see Texas skies still o'er me.

Now fuller and truer the coastline shows –
Was ever a scene so splendid?
I feel the breath of the Munster breeze;
Thank God that my exile's ended!
Old scenes, old songs, old friends again,
The vale and the cot I was born in –
O Ireland! up from my heart of hearts
I bid you the top of the morning.

The Wind that Shakes the Barley

Katharine Tynan (1861–1931)

There's music in my heart all day;
I hear it late and early;
It comes from fields and far away,
The wind that shakes the barley.

Above the uplands drenched with dew,
The sky hangs soft and pearly;
The emerald world is listening to
The wind that shakes the barley.

Above the bluest mountain crest,
The lark is singing rarely;
It rocks the singer into rest,
The wind that shakes the barley.

Oh, still through summers and through springs,
It calls me late and early.
Come home, come home, come home, it sings,
The wind that shakes the barley.

Off to Philadelphia

County Mayo

Anon

Far away from the land of the shamrock and heather,
In search of a living, as exiles we roam,
But whenever we chance to assemble together,
We think of the land where we once had a home.
But these homes are destroyed and our soil confiscated,
The hand of the tyrant brought plunder and woe,
The fires are now quenched and our hearts desolated,
In our once happy homes in the County Mayo.

Long years have now passed since with hearts full of sorrow,
The land of the shamrock we left far behind,
But how we would like to go back there tomorrow,
To the scenes of our youth, which we still bear in mind;
The days of our childhood, it's now we recall them,
They cling to our vision wherever we go;
And the friends of our youth we will never forget them,
They too are exiled from the County Mayo.

From Galway to Dublin, from Derry to Kerry,
New York and 'Frisco and Boston also,
In Pittsburgh, Chicago, Detroit and Toronto,
There are stout-hearted men from the County Mayo,
Now boys, stick together whatever the weather,
Ne'er show the white feather wherever ye go.
Be like a brother and help one another,
Like the true-hearted men from the County Mayo.

Off to Philadelphia

Anon

Oh, me name is Paddy Leary from a spot in Tipperary,
The hearts of all the girls I'm a thorn in,
But come the break of dawnin' it is they who'll be forlorn,
For I'm off to Philadelphia in the morning,

Chorus
With me bundle on me shoulder, faith, there's no man can be bolder,
I'm leaving dear old Ireland without warning,
For I lately took the notion for to cross the briny ocean,
And I'm off to Philadelphia in the morning.

There's a girl named Kate Malone sure I'd hoped to call me own,
To see my little cabin floor adornin',
But my heart is sad and weary, how can she be Mrs Leary?
When I'm off to Philadelphia in the morning.

When they told me I must leave the place I tried to wear a cheerful face,
To show me heart's deep sorrow I was scornin',
But the tears will surely blind me for the friends I leave behind me,
When I'm off to Philadelphia in the morning.

Final Chorus
With me bundle on me shoulder sure there's no man can be bolder,
I'm leaving just the spot that I was born in,
But some day I'll take the notion to come back across that ocean,
To my home in dear old Ireland in the morning.

Goodbye, Mursheen Durkin

Anon

In the days I went a courtin',
I was never tired resortin',
To the alehouse and the playhouse and many a house beside.
But I told my brother Séamus,
I'll be off now and grow famous,
And before I come home again, I'll roam the world wide.

Chorus
So goodbye, Mursheen Durkin,
Sure I'm sick and tired of workin'.
No more I'll dig the praties, no longer I'll be fooled,
But as sure as my name is Carney,
I'll be off to Californy,
And instead of digging praties, I'll be diggin' lumps of gold.

Oh! I courted girls in Blarney,
In Kanturk and in Killarney,
In Passage and in Queenstown – I mean the Cove of Cork.
But I'm tired of all this pleasure,
So now I'll take my leisure,
And the next time that you hear, 'twill be a letter from New York.

Goodbye Mick

Anon

The ship it sails in half an hour to cross the broad Atlantic,
My friends are standing on the quay with grief and sorrow frantic.
I'm just about to sail away in the good ship Dan O'Leary,
The anchor's weighed and the gangway's up, I'm leaving Tipperary.

Chorus
And it's goodbye Mick and goodbye Pat and goodbye Kate and Mary,
The anchor's weighed and the gangway's up, I'm leaving Tipperary.
And now the steam is blowing off, I have no more to say.
I'm bound for New York City, boys, three thousand miles away.

In my portmanteau here I have some cabbage, beans and bacon,
And if you think I can't eat that, well, there's where yer mistaken.
For this ship will play with pitch and toss for half a dozen farthings,
I'll roll me bundle on me back and walk to Castle Gardens.

Now I won't come that Yankee chat, I guess I'm calculatin',
Come liquor up old sonny boy, when an old friend I am treatin'.
I'm deep in love with Molly Burke like an ass is fond of clover,
I'll send for her when I get there – that's if she will come over.

Then fare thee well old Erin dear, to part me heart does ache well,
From Carrickfergus to Cape Clear – I'll never see your equal.
Although to foreign parts we're bound where cannibals may eat us,
We'll ne'er forget the Holy Ground of poteen and potatoes.

When good St Paddy banished snakes he shook them from his garment,
He never thought we'd go abroad to look upon such vermint.
Nor quit this land where whiskey grew to wear the Yankee button,
Take vinegar for mountain dew and toads for mountain mutton.

The Shores of Amerikay

Anon

I'm bidding farewell to the land of my youth,
And the home I love so well.
And the mountains so grand round my own native land,
I'm bidding them all farewell.
With an aching heart I'll bid them adieu,
For tomorrow I'll sail far away.
O'er the raging foam for to seek a home,
On the shores of Amerikay.

It's not for the want of employment I'm going,
It's not for the love of fame.
That fortune bright may shine over me,
And give me a glorious name.
It's not for the want of employment I'm going,
O'er the weary and stormy sea,
But to seek a home for my own true love,
On the shores of Amerikay.

And when I am bidding my last farewell,
The tears like rain will blind.
To think of my friends in my own native land,
and the home I'm leaving behind.
But if I'm to die in a foreign land,
And be buried so far far away,
No fond mother's tears will be shed o'er my grave,
On the shores of Amerikay.

The Irish Emigrant

Lady Dufferin (1807–67)

I'm sittin' on the stile, Mary,
Where we sat side by side,
On a bright May mornin' long ago,
When first you were my bride:
The corn was springin' fresh and green,
And the lark sang loud and high –
And the red was on your lip, Mary,
And the love-light in your eye.

The place is little changed, Mary.
The day is bright as then.
The lark's loud song is in my ear,
And the corn is green again;
But I miss the soft clasp of your hand,
And your breath warm on my cheek,
And I still keep listening for the words,
You never more will speak.

'Tis but a step down yonder lane,
And the little church stands near –
The church where we were wed, Mary,
I see the spire from here.
And the graveyard lies between, Mary,
And my step might break your rest –
For I've laid you, darling, down to sleep,
With your baby on your breast.

I'm very lonely now, Mary,
For the poor make no new friends;
But, oh, they love the better still,
The few our Father sends!
And you were all I had, Mary,
My blessin' and my pride!
There's nothing left to care for now,
Since my poor Mary died.

Yours was the good, brave heart, Mary,
That still kept hoping on,
When the trust in God had left my soul,
And my arm's young strength was gone.
There was comfort ever on your lip,
And the kind look on your brow –
I bless you, Mary, for that same,
Though you cannot hear me now.

I thank you for your patient smile,
When your heart was fit to break,
When the hunger pain was gnawin' there,
And you hid it for my sake.
I bless you for the pleasant word,
When your heart was sad and sore –
Oh! I'm thankful you are gone, Mary,
Where grief can't reach you more.

I'm biddin' you a long farewell,
My Mary – kind and true!
But I'll not forget you, darling,
In the land I'm goin' to.
They say there's bread and work for all,
And the sun shines always there –
But I'll not forget old Ireland,
Were it fifty times as fair!

And often in these grand old woods,
I'll sit and shut my eyes,
And my heart will travel back again,
To the place where Mary lies;
And I'll think I see the little stile,
Where we sat side by side,
And the springing corn and the bright May morn,
When first you were my bride.

Teddy O'Neale

James Gaspard Maedar (1809–76)

I've come to the cabin he danced his wild jigs in,
As neat a mud cabin as ever was seen.
And consid'rin' it served to keep poultry and pigs in,
I'm sure it was always most elegant clean!
But now, all about seems so sad and so dreary,
All sad and all silent, no piper, no reel;
Not even the sun through the casement is cheery,
Since I lost my own darling boy, Teddy O'Neale.

I dreamt but last night (Oh bad luck to my dreaming),
I'd die if I thought 'twould come surely to pass,
But I dreamt while the tears down my pillow were streaming,
That Teddy was courting another fair lass.
Och did I not wake with a weeping and wailing,
The grief of that thought was too deep to conceal.
My mother cried, 'Norah, child, what is your ailing?'
And all I could utter was, 'Teddy O'Neale.'

Shall I ever forget when the big ship was ready.
The moment had come when my love must depart.
How I sobbed like a spalpeen, 'Goodbye to you, Teddy.'
With drops on my cheek and a stone in my heart.
He says 'tis to better his fortune he's roving,
But what would be gold to the joy I would feel,
If I saw him come back to me honest and loving,
Still poor but my own darling Teddy O'Neale.

The Moon behind the Hill

William Kenneally (1828–76)

I watched last night the rising moon
Upon a foreign strand,
Till mem'ries came like flowers of June,
Of home and fatherland,
I dreamt I was a child once more,
Beside the rippling rill,
When first I saw, in days of yore,
The moon behind the hill.

It brought me back the visions grand,
That purpled boyhood's dreams,
Its youthful loves, its happy land,
As bright as morning beams,
It brought me back my own sweet Nore,
The castle and the mill,
Until my eyes could see no more,
The moon behind the hill.

It brought me back a mother's love,
Until, in accents wild,
I prayed her from her home above,
To guard her lonely child,
It brought me one across the wave,
To live in mem'ry still,
It brought me back my Kathleen's grave,
The moon behind the hill.

And there, beneath the silv'ry sky,
I lived life o'er again,
I counted all its hopes gone by,
I wept at all its pain.
And when I'm gone, oh! may some tongue,
The minstrel's wish fulfil,
And still remember him who sang,
'The Moon Behind the Hill'.

I'll Take You Home Again, Kathleen

Thomas P. Westendorf (1848–1923)

I'll take you home again, Kathleen,
Across the ocean wild and wide,
To where your heart has ever been,
Since first you were my bonny bride.
The roses all have left your cheeks,
I've watched them fade away and die,
Your voice is sad when'er you speak,
And tears bedim your loving eyes.

Chorus
Oh, I will take you back, Kathleen,
To where your heart will feel no pain,
And when the fields are fresh and green,
I will take you to your home, Kathleen.

I know you love me, Kathleen dear,
Your heart was ever fond and true.
I always feel when you are near,
That life holds nothing dear but you.
The smiles that once you gave to me,
I scarcely ever see them now.
But many many times I've seen,
A darkening shadow on your brow.

The Emigrant's Letter

Percy French (1854–1920)

Dear Danny:
I'm taking the pen in my hand,
To tell you we're just out o' sight o' the land;
In the grand Allen liner we're sailing in style,
But we're sailing away from the Emerald Isle.
And a long sort of sigh seemed to rise from us all,
As the waves hid the last bit of ould Donegal.
Och! it's well to be you that is takin' your tay,
Where they're cutting the corn down in Creeshlough the day.

I spoke to the captain – he won't turn her round,
And if I swum back I'd be apt to be drowned.
I'll stay where I am, for the diet is great,
The best of combustibles piled on me plate
But though it is 'sumpchus' I'd swap the whole lot,
For the ould wooden spoon and the stirabout pot,
And Katey forninst me a-wettin' the tay,
Where they're cutting the corn down in Creeshlough the day.

There's a woman on board who knows Katey by sight,
So we talked of old times till they put out the light.
I'm to meet the good woman tomorra on deck,
And we'll talk about Katey from this to Quebec.
I know I'm no match for her – oh! not in the least,
With her house and two cows, and her brother a priest,
But the woman declares Katey's heart's on the say,
And mine's back with Katey in Creeshlough the day.

If Katey is courted by Patsey or Mick,
Put a word in for me with a lump of a stick.
Don't kill Patsey outright; he has no sort of chance,
But Mickey's a rogue you might murder at wance;
For Katey might think, as the longer she waits,
A boy in the hand is worth two in the States:

And she'll promise to honour, to love and obey,
Some robber that's roamin' round Creeshlough the day.

Goodbye to you, Dan, there' no more to be said,
And I think the salt wather's got's into me head,
For it dhreeps from me eyes when I call to me mind,
The friends and the colleen I'm leavin' behind.
But still she might wait; whin I bid her goodbye,
There was just the last taste of a tear in her eye,
And a break in her voice when she said, 'You might stay.
But, please God, you'll come back to ould Creeshlough some day.'

The Old Bog Road

Teresa Brayton (1868–1943)

My feet are here on Broadway this blessed harvest morn,
But oh the ache that's in me for the spot where I was born.
My weary hands are blistered from toil in cold and heat,
But oh to swing a scythe today through a field of Irish wheat.
If I'd the chance to wander back or own a king's abode,
I'd sooner see the hawthorn tree on the old bog road.

My mother died last springtime when Erin's fields were green,
The neighbours said her waking was the finest ever seen.
There were snowdrops and primroses all piled beside her bed,
And Ferns's church was crowded as her funeral Mass was said,
But here was I on Broadway a-building bricks per load,
As they carried out her coffin down the old bog road,

Now life's a weary puzzle, past finding out by man,
I take the day for what it's worth and do the best I can.
If no one cares a rush for me what need to make a moan,
I'll go my way and earn my pay and smoke my pipe alone.
Each human heart must bear its grief though bitter be the 'bode,
O God be with you, Ireland, and the old bog road.

Four Ducks on a Pond

I'll Tell Me Ma

Anon

I'll tell me ma when I go home,
The boys won't leave the girls alone;
They pull my hair; they steal my comb,
But that's all right till I go home.
She is handsome; she is pretty;
She is the belle of Belfast city;
She is coortin' one, two, three,
Please won't you tell me who is he?

Albert Mooney says he loves her;
All the boys are fighting for her.
They rap at the door and they ring the bell,
Saying, 'O my true love are you well?'
Out she comes as white as snow,
Rings on her fingers, bells on her toes.
Old Johnny Murray says she'll die
If she doesn't get the fellow with the roving eye.

Let the wind and the rain and the breeze blow high,
And the snow come falling from the sky,
She's as nice as apple pie,
And she'll have her own lad by and by.
One young man is fighting for her,
All the rest they swear they'll have her,
Let them all say as they will,
Albert Mooney loves her still.

Hughes's Bread

Anon

A tribute to the Belfast baker Bernard Hughes (1808–78), whose cheap baps killed hunger during the Famine years and after.

Barney Hughes's bread
Sticks to your belly like lead.
It's no wonder
You fart like thunder.
Barney Hughes's bread.

My Aunt Jane

Anon

My Aunt Jane, she took me in,
She gave me tea out o' her wee tin,
Half a bap and a wee snow top,
And cinnamon buds out o' her wee shop.

My Aunt Jane has a bell at the door,
A white step-stone and a clean-swept floor,
Candy apples and hard green pears,
And conversation lozengers.

My Aunt Jane can dance a jig,
And sing a ballad round a sweetie pig,
Wee red eyes and a cord for a tail,
Hanging in a bunch from a farthing nail.

My Aunt Jane, she's awful smart,
She bakes a ring in an apple tart,
And when that Hallowe'en comes around,
Fornenst that tart I'm always found.

Our Wee School

Anon

Our wee school's a nice wee school,
Made of brick and plaster.
The only thing that we don't like,
Is the baldy-headed master.

He goes to the pub on Saturday night;
He goes to Mass on Sunday.
To pray to God to give him strength,
To slaughter us on Monday.

A Ballad of Master McGrath

Anon

*The story of Ireland's most famous greyhound, that won the Waterloo Cup
in 1868, 1869 and 1870.*

Eighteen sixty-nine being the date of the year,
Those Waterloo sportsmen and more did appear,
For to gain the great prizes and bear them awa',
Never counting on Ireland and Master McGrath.

On the twelfth of December, that day of renown,
McGrath and his keeper they left Lurgan town:
A gale in the Channel it soon drove them o'er.
On the thirteenth they landed on fair England's shore.

And when they arrived there in big London town,
Those great English sportsmen they all gathered round –
And some of the gentlemen gave a 'Ha! Ha!'
Saying: 'Is that the great dog you call Master McGrath?'

And one of those gentlemen standing around,
Says: 'I don't give a damn for your Irish greyhound.'
And another he laughs with a scornful 'Ha! Ha!
We'll soon humble the pride of your Master McGrath.'

Then Lord Lurgan came forward and said: 'Gentlemen,
If there's any amongst you has money to spend –
For you nobles of England I don't care a straw –
Here's five thousand to one upon Master McGrath.'

Then McGrath he looked up and he wagged his old tail,
Informing his lordship, 'I know what you mane.
Don't fear noble Brownlow, don't fear them, agra.
For I'll tarnish their laurels,' said Master McGrath.

And Rose stood uncovered, the great English pride,
Her master and keeper were close by her side;
They have let her away and the crowd cried, 'Hurrah!'
For the pride of all England – and Master McGrath.

As Rose and the Master they both ran along.
'Now I wonder,' says Rose, 'what took you from your home.
You should have stopped there in your Irish demesne,
And not come to gain laurels on Albion's plain.'

'Well, I know,' says McGrath, 'we have wild heather bogs
But you'll find in old Ireland there's good men and dogs.
Lead on, bold Britannia; give none of your jaw,
Snuff that up your nostrils,' says Master McGrath.

Then the hare she went on just as the swift as the wind.
He was sometimes before her and sometimes behind.
Rose gave the first turn according to law;
But the second was given by Master McGrath.

The hare she led on with a wonderful view,
And swift as the wind o'er the green field she flew.
But he jumped on her back and he held up his paw.
'Three cheers for old Ireland,' says Master McGrath.

Doran's Ass

Anon

One Paddy Doyle lived near Killarney,
And loved a maid called Betty Toole;
His tongue, I own, was tipped with blarney,
Which seemed to him a golden rule.
From day to dawn he watched his colleen,
And often to himself would say:
'What need I care? Sure here's my darling,
Advancing to meet me on the way.'

Chorus
Whack fol de darral ido.
Whack fol de darral lal do.

One heavenly night in last November,
The moon shone gently from above.
What night it was I don't remember,
But Paddy went to meet his love.
That day Paddy took some liquor,
Which made his spirits light and gay.
Says he, 'Where's the use in me walking quicker?
Don't I know she'll meet me on the way.'

So he tuned his pipe and fell a-humming,
As slowly onward he did creep,
But fatigue and whiskey soon overcame him
And down he lay and fell asleep.
But he was not long without a comrade,
And one that could kick up the hay,
For a big jackass soon smelled out Pat,
And lay down beside him on the way.

Pat stretched his arms on the grass,
Thinking of his little dear.
He dreamt of comforts without number,
Coming on in the ensuing year.

He stretched his arms on the grass;
His spirits felt so light and gay,
But instead of Bet he gripped the ass,
And he roared: 'I have her anyway.'

He hugged and smugged his hairy messer,
And flung his hat to heavenly care.
Says Pat: 'She's mine and may heaven bless her,
But, oh, be my soul, she's like a bear.'
He put his hands on the donkey's nose;
With that the ass began to bray;
Pat jumped up and roared out:
'Who sarved me in such a way?'

Like blazes then away he cut,
At railway speed or as fast I'm sure,
But he never stopt a leg or foot,
Until he came to Betty's door.
By this time now 'twas dawning morning,
So down on his knees he fell to pray,
Saying: 'Let me in, och Betty darlin',
For I'm kilt and murdered on the way.'

So up and told her all quite civil,
While she prepared a burned glass,
How he had hugged and smugged the devil.
Says she: 'Sure that was Doran's ass.'
'And I believe it was,' says Pat.
They both got wed on the ensuing day,
But he never got back that new straw hat,
That the jackass ate up on the way.

An Elegy on the Death of a Mad Dog

Oliver Goldsmith (1724–72)

Good people all, of every sort,
Give ear unto my song;
And if you find it wondrous short,
It cannot hold you long.

In Islington there was a man,
Of whom the world might say,
That still a godly race he ran,
Whene'er he went to pray.

A kind and gentle heart he had,
To comfort friends and foes;
The naked every day he clad,
When he put on his clothes.

And in that town a dog was found,
As many dog there be,
Both mongrel, puppy, whelp and hound,
And curs of low degree.

This dog and man at first were friends,
But when a pique began,
The dog, to gain some private ends,
Went mad and bit the man.

Around from all the neighbouring streets,
The wond'ring neighbours ran,
And swore the dog had lost its wits,
To bite so good a man.

The wound it seemed both sore and sad,
To every Christian eye,
And while they swore the dog was mad,
They swore the man would die.

But soon a wonder came to light,
That showed the rogues they lied.
The man recovered from the bite;
The dog it was that died.

The Angels' Whisper

Samuel Lover (1797–1868)

A baby was sleeping; its mother was weeping,
For her husband was far on the wild raging sea;
And the tempest was swelling round the fisherman's dwelling.
And she cried, 'Dermot, darling, oh! come back to me.'

Her beads while she numbered, the baby still slumbered,
And smiled in her face, as she bended her knee:
'Oh bless'd be that warning, my child, thy sleep adorning,
For I know that the angels are whispering with thee.'

'And while they are keeping bright watch o'er thy sleeping,
Oh pray to them softly, my baby, with me;
And say thou wouldst rather they'd watch o'er thy father,
For I know that the angels are whispering with thee.'

The dawn of the morning saw Dermot returning.
And the wife wept with joy her babe's father to see;
And closely caressing her child with a blessing,
She said, 'I knew that the angels were whispering with thee.'

Caoch the Piper

John Keegan (1809-49)

One winter's day, long, long ago,
When I was a little fellow,
A piper wandered to our door,
Grey-headed, blind and yellow:
And, oh! how glad was my young heart,
Though earth and sky looked dreary,
To see the stranger and his dog –
Poor Pinch and Caoch O'Leary.

And when he stowed away his 'bag',
Cross-barred with green and yellow,
I thought and said, 'In Ireland's ground,
There's not so fine a fellow.'
And Fineen Burke and Shaun Magee,
And Eily, Kate and Mary,
Rushed in, with panting haste, to see,
And welcome Caoch O'Leary.

O! God be with those happy times!
O! God be with my childhood!
When I, bare-headed, roamed all day –
Bird-nesting in the wild wood,
I'll not forget those sunny hours,
However years may vary;
I'll not forget my early friends,
Nor honest Caoch O'Leary.

Poor Caoch and Pinch slept well that night,
And in the morning early,
He called me up to hear him play
'The Wind that Shakes the Barley';
And then he stroked my flaxen hair,
And cried, 'God mark, my deary!'
And how I wept when he said, 'Farewell,
And think of Caoch O'Leary.'

And seasons came and went and still,
Old Caoch was not forgotten,
Although we thought him dead and gone,
And in the cold grave rotten;
And often, when I walked and talked,
With Eily, Kate and Mary,
We thought of childhood's rosy hours,
And prayed for Caoch O'Leary.

Well – twenty summers had gone past,
And June's red sun was sinking,
When I, a man, sat by my door,
Of twenty sad things thinking.
A little dog came up the way,
His gait was slow and weary,
And at his tail a lame man limped, –
'Twas Pinch and Caoch O'Leary!

Old Caoch, but, oh! how woebegone!
His form is bowed and bending,
His fleshless hands are stiff and wan,
Ay – time is even blending,
The colours on his threadbare 'bag'
And Pinch is twice as hairy,
And 'thin-spare' as when first I saw,
Himself and Caoch O'Leary.

God's blessing here!' the wanderer cried,
'Far, far be hell's black viper;
Does anybody hereabouts,
Remember Caoch the Piper?'
With swelling heart I grasped his hand;
The old man murmured, 'Deary,
Are you the silky-headed child,
That loved poor Caoch O'Leary?

'Yes, yes,' I said – the wanderer wept,
As if his heart was breaking –
'And where, a vic machree,' he sobbed,

'Is all the merrymaking
I found here twenty years ago?'
'My tale,' I sighed, 'might weary;
Enough to say – there's none but me,
To welcome Caoch O'Leary.'

'Vo, vo, vo!' the old man cried,
And wrung his hands in sorrow,
'Pray let me in, astór machree,
And I'll go home tomorrow.
My peace is made; I'll calmly leave,
This world so cold and dreary;
And you shall keep my pipes and dog,
And pray for Caoch O'Leary.'

With Pinch I watched his bed that night;
Next day his wish was granted:
He died; and Father James was brought,
And the requiem Mass was chanted.
The neighbours came; we dug his grave,
Near Eily, Kate and Mary,
And there he sleeps his last sweet sleep.
God rest you! Caoch O'Leary.

The Irish Wolfhound

Denis Florence MacCarthy (1817–82)

His stature tall, his body long,
His back like night, his breast like snow,
His foreleg pillar-like and strong,
His hind leg like a bended bow;
Rough curling hair, head long and thin,
His ear a leaf so small and round;
Not Bran, the favourite dog of Finn,
Could rival John MacDonnell's hound.

As fly the shadows o'er the grass,
He flies with step as light and sure,
He hunts the wolf through Tostan pass,
And starts the deer by Lisanoure.
The music of the Sabbath bells,
O Con, has not a sweeter sound,
Than when along the valley swells,
The cry of John MacDonnell's hound.

Four Ducks on a Pond

William Allingham (1824–89)

Four ducks on a pond,
A grass-bank beyond,
A blue sky of spring,
White clouds on the wing.
What a little thing,
To remember for years –
To remember with tears.

The Monk and his White Cat

(from the Irish)
Alfred Perceval Graves (1846–1931)

Pangar, my white cat and I,
Silent ply our special crafts;
Hunting mice his one pursuit,
Mine to shoot keen spirit shafts.

Rest I love, all fame beyond,
In the bond of some rare book;
Yet white Pangar from his play,
Casts, my way, no jealous look.

Thus alone within one cell,
Safe we dwell – not dull the tale –
Since his ever favourite sport,
Each to court will never fail.

Now a mouse, to swell his spoils,
In his toils he spears with skill;
Now a meaning deeply thought,
I have caught with startled thrill.

Now his green full-shining gaze,
Darts its rays against the wall;
Now my feebler glances mark,
Through the dark bright knowledge fall.

Leaping up with joyful purr,
In mouse fur his sharp claw sticks,
Problems difficult and dear,
With my spear I, too, transfix.

Crossing not each other's will,
Diverse still, yet still allied,
Following each his lone ends,
Constant friends we here abide.

Pangar, master of his art,
Plays his part in pranksome youth;
While, in age sedate, I clear,
Shadows from the sphere of truth.

Sweet Marie

Percy French (1854–1920)

I've a little racin' mare called Sweet Marie,
And the temper of a bear has Sweet Marie,
But I've backed the mare to win and on her I've all my tin;
So we'll take a trial spin, Sweet Marie.

Chorus
Hould your hoult, Sweet Marie,
If you bolt, Sweet Marie,
Sure you'll never win the Farmer's Cup for me;
And if you don't pull it through, faith I'm done and so are you,
For I'll trade you off for glue, Sweet Marie.

Now the colours that I chose for Sweet Marie,
Were lavender and rose for Sweet Marie.
Och, but now, no thanks to you, sure I'm quite another hue,
For I'm only black and blue, Sweet Marie.

Chorus
Hould your hoult, Sweet Marie,
If you bolt, Sweet Marie,
Sure you'll never win the Farmer's Cup for me;
Every daisy in the dell ought to know me pretty well,
For on every one I fell, Sweet Marie.

Now we're started for the Cup, my Sweet Marie,
Weight for age and owners up, my Sweet Marie.
Owners up just now, I own, but the way you're waltzin' roun'
Sure, 'twill soon be owners down, Sweet Marie.

Chorus
Hould your hoult, Sweet Marie,
Pass the colt, Sweet Marie,
Och you've gone and lost the Farmer's Cup for me;
You're a stayer too, I find: but you're not the proper kind
For you stay too far behind, Sweet Marie.

Sheep and Lambs

Katharine Tynan (1861–1931)

All in the April morning,
April airs were abroad.
The sheep with their little lambs,
Passed me by on the road.
The sheep with their little lambs,
Passed me by on the road.
All in the April evening,
I thought on the Lamb of God.

The lambs were weary and crying,
With a weak human cry.
I thought on the Lamb of God,
Going meekly to die.
Up in the blue, blue mountains,
Dewy pastures are sweet.
Rest for the little bodies,
Rest for the little feet.

Rest for the Lamb of God,
Up on the hill-top green,
Only a cross of shame,
Two stark crosses between.
All in the April evening,
April airs were abroad.
I saw the sheep with their lambs,
And thought on the Lamb of God.

The Wild Swans at Coole

William Butler Yeats (1865–1939)

The trees are in their autumn beauty,
The woodland paths are dry,
Under the October twilight the water
Mirrors a still sky;
Upon the brimming water among the stones
Are nine-and-fifty swans.

The nineteenth autumn has come upon me
Since I first made my count;
I saw, before I had well finished
All suddenly mount
And scatter wheeling in great broken rings
Upon their clamorous wings.

I have looked upon these brilliant creatures
And now my heart is sore.
All's changed since I, hearing at twilight,
The first time upon this shore,
The bell-beat of their wings above my head,
Trod with a lighter tread.

Unwearied still, lover by lover,
They paddle in the cold
Companionable streams or climb the air;
Their hearts have not grown old;
Passion or conquest, wander where they will,
Attend upon them still.

But now they drift upon the still water,
Mysterious, beautiful;
Among what rushes will they build,
By what lake's edge or pool
Delight men's eyes when I awake some day,
To find they have flown away.

The Cat and the Moon

William Butler Yeats (1865–1939)

The cat went here and there
And the moon spun round like a top,
And the nearest kin of the moon,
The creeping cat, looked up.
Black Minnaloushe stared at the moon,
For, wander and wail as he would,
The pure cold light in the sky
Troubled his animal blood.
Minnaloushe runs in the grass
Lifting his delicate feet.
Do you dance, Minnaloushe, do you dance?
When two close kindred meet,
What better than call a dance?
Maybe the moon may learn,
Tired of that courtly fashion,
A new dance turn.
Minnaloushe creeps through the grass
From moonlit place to place.
The sacred moon overhead
Has taken a new phase.
Does Minnaloushe know that his pupils
Will pass from change to change,
And that from round to crescent,
From crescent to round they range?
Minnaloushe creeps through the grass
Alone, and important and wise,
And lifts to the changing moon
His changing eyes.

Wee Hughie

'Elizabeth Shane' (Gertrude Hind) (1877–1951)

He's gone to school; Wee Hughie,
An' him not four.
Sure I saw the fright was in him,
When he left the door.
But he took a hand of Denny,
An' a hand of Dan,
Wi' Joe's owld coat upon him –
Och, the poor wee man!

He cut the quarest figure,
More stout than thin,
And trottin' right an' steady,
Wi' his toes turned in.
I watched him to the corner,
O' the big turf stack
An' the more his feet went forrit,
Still his head turned back.

He was lookin' would I call him,
Och, me heart was woe –
Sure it's lost I am without him,
But he be to go.
I followed to the turnin';
When he passed it by,
God help him, he was cryin',
And maybe so was I.

Padric the Fidiler

Pádraic Gregory (1886–1962)

Padric sits in the garden,
Inundher the bright new moon,
An' from his fidil coaxes,
A lovely, dreamy tune.

Och. I love the tune he's playin',
An' wisht it was for me,
But I know it's for the birdeens,
Up in the cherry tree.

Sure, iv'ry night they peep from,
Inundher their mother's wings,
Tae hear the silvery music,
His wee dark fidil sings.

An' for them he's always playin',
An' has nae thought o' me;
For if I go out he wanders,
Away from the cherry tree.

Let Us Be Merry

Let Him Go, Let Him Tarry

Anon

Farewell to cold winter; summer's come at last;
Nothing have I gained but my true love I have lost.
I'll sing and I'll be happy like the birds upon the tree,
But since he deceived me I care no more for he.

Chorus
Let him go, let him tarry,
Let him sink or let him swim.
He doesn't care for me nor I don't care for him.
He can go and get another that I hope he will enjoy,
For I'm going to marry a far nicer boy.

He wrote me a letter saying he was very bad.
I sent him back an answer saying I was awful glad.
He wrote to me another saying he was well and strong,
But I care no more about him than the ground he walks upon.

Some of his friends they had a very good wish for me.
Others of his friends, they could hang me on a tree;
But soon I'll let them see my love and soon I'll let them know,
That I can get a new sweetheart on any ground I go.

He can go to his old mother and set her mind at ease.
I hear she is an old, old woman, very hard to please.
It's slighting me and talking ill is what she's always done,
Because that I was courting her great big ugly son.

The Maid of the Sweet Brown Knowe

Anon

Come all, ye lads and lasses and hear my mournful tale.
Ye tender hearts that weep for love to sigh you will not fail.
'Tis all about a young man and my song will tell you how,
He lately came a-courting of the Maid of the Sweet Brown Knowe.

Said he, 'My pretty fair maid, could you and I agree,
To join our hands in wedlock bands and married we will be.
We'll join our hands in wedlock bands and you'll have my plighted vow,
That I'll do my whole endeavours for the Maid of the Sweet Brown
      Knowe.

Now this young and pretty fickle thing, she knew not what to say.
Her eyes did shine like silver bright and merrily did play.
Says she, 'Young man, your love subdue; I am not ready now.
And I'll spend another season at the foot of the Sweet Brown Knowe.'

'Oh,' says he, 'My pretty fair maid, now why do you say so?
Look down in yonder valley where my verdant crops do grow.
Look down in yonder valley at my horses and my plough,
All at their daily labour for the Maid of the Sweet Brown Knowe.

'If they're at their daily labour, kind sir, it is not for me.
I've heard of your behaviour, I have, kind sir,' said she.
'There is an inn where you drop in, I've heard the people say,
Where you rap and you call and you pay for all and go home at the dawn
     of day.'

'If I rap and call and pay for all, my money is all my own.
I never spent aught of your fortune for I hear that you have none.
You thought you had my poor heart broke in talking to me now,
But I'll leave you where I found you at the foot of the Sweet Brown
      Knowe.

Brian O'Linn

Anon

Brian O'Linn was a gentleman born.
His hair it was long and his beard unshorn.
His teeth were out and his eyes far in –
'I'm a wonderful beauty,' says Brian O'Linn!

Brian O'Linn was hard up for a coat.
He borrowed the skin of a neighbouring goat.
He buckled the horns right under his chin –
'They'll answer for pistols,' says Brian O'Linn.

Brian O'Linn had no breeches to wear.
He got him a sheepskin to make him a pair
With the fleshy side out and the woolly side in –
'They are pleasant and cool,' says Brian O'Linn.

Brian O'Linn had no hat on his head,
He stuck on a pot that was under the shed.
He murdered a cod for the sake of his fin –
''Twill pass for a feather,' says Brian O'Linn.

Brian O'Linn had no shirt on his back.
He went to a neighbour and borrowed a sack.
He puckered a meal-bag under his chin –
'They'll take it for ruffles,' says Brian O'Linn.

Brian O'Linn had no shoes at all.
He brought an old pair at a cobbler's stall.
The uppers were broke and the soles were thin –
'They'll do me for dancing,' says Brian O'Linn.

Brian O'Linn had no watch for to wear.
He bought a fine turnip and scooped it out fair.
He slipped a live cricket right under the skin –
'They'll think it is ticking,' says Brian O'Linn.

Brian O'Linn was in want of a brooch.
He stuck a brass pin in a big cockroach.
The breast of his shirt he fixed it straight in –
'They'll think it's a diamond,' says Brian O'Linn.

Brian O'Linn went a-courting one night.
He set both the mother and daughter to fight –
'Stop, stop,' he exclaimed, 'if you have but the tin.
I'll marry you both,' says Brian O'Linn.

Brian O'Linn went to bring his wife home.
He had but one horse that was all skin and bone –
'I'll put her behind me, as nate as a pin,
And her mother before me,' says Brian O'Linn.

Brian O'Linn and his wife and wife's mother,
They all crossed over the bridge together.
The bridge broke down and they all tumbled in –
'We'll go home by water,' says Brian O'Linn.

The Agricultural Irish Girl

Anon

If all the women in the town were bundled up together,
I know a girl could beat them, in any kind of weather;
The rain can't wash the powder off because she does not wear it.
Her face and figure are all her own: it's true, I can declare it.

Chorus
For she's a big stout lump of an agricultural Irish girl.
She neither paints nor powders and her figure is all her own,
And she can strike that hard that you'd think that you'd
*   been struck by the kick of a mule.*
It's the 'full of the house' of Irish love is Mary Ann Malone.

She was only seventeen last grass and still improving greatly.
I wonder what she will be like when her bones are set completely.
You'd think your hand was in a vice the moment that she shakes it,
And if there's any cake around it's Mary Ann that takes it.

The Ould Orange Flute

Anon

In the County Tyrone, near the town of Dungannon,
Where many's the ruction myself had a han' in,
Bob Williamson lived, a weaver by trade,
And we all of us thought him a stout Orange blade.
On the Twelfth of July, as it yearly did come,
Bob played on the flute to the sound of the drum;
You may talk of your harp, your piano or lute,
But there's none could compare with the ould Orange flute.

But the sinful deceiver he took us all in,
And married a Papish called Brigid McGinn,
Turned Papish himself and forsook the ould cause,
That gave us our freedom, religion and laws.
Now the boys of the place made some comment upon it,
And Bob had to fly to the province of Connacht:
He flew with his wife and fixtures to boot,
And along with the rest went the ould Orange flute.

At the chapel on Sundays to atone for his past deeds,
He said Paters and Aves and counted his brown beads,
And after a while at the priest's own desire,
He took the ould flute for to play in the choir.
He took the ould flute for to play at the Mass,
But the instrument shivered and sighed, 'Oh, Alas!'
And blow as he would, though he made a great noise
The flute would play only 'The Protestant Boys'.

Bob flustered and fingered and got in a splatter,
And dipped the ould flute in the blessed holy water.
He thought that the dipping would bring a new sound;
When he blew it again it played 'Croppies, Lie Down'.
He could whistle his utmost and finger and blow,
To play Papish tunes, but the flute wouldn't go.
'Kick the Pope', 'The Boyne Water' and 'Croppies, Lie Down'
And no Papish squeak in it all could be found.

At the council of priests that was held the next day,
'Twas decided to banish the ould flute away.
Since they couldn't knock heresy out of its head,
They bought Bob a new one to play in its stead.
So the ould flute was doomed and its fate was pathetic;
'Twas sentenced and burned at the stake as heretic.
As the flames roared around it they heard a strange noise:
The ould flute was still playing 'The Protestant Boys'.

Killyburn Brae

Anon

It's true that the women are worse than the men.
Right fol right fol tiddy fol lay;
It's true that the women are worse than the men.
They went down to Hell and were thrown out again,

Chorus
With your right fol lol tiddy fol lol.
Fol the dol lol the lol, lol the doll ay.

There was an old man lived at Killyburn Brae.
Right fol right fol tiddy fol lay;
There was an old man lived at Killyburn Brae.
And he had a wife was the plague of his days.

The divil he came to the man at the plough.
Right fol right fol tiddy fol lay;
The divil he came to the man at the plough.
Saying, 'One of your family I must take now.'

Said he, 'My good man, I have come for your wife.'
Right fol right fol tiddy fol lay;
Said he, 'My good man, I have come for your wife.
For I hear she's the plague and torment of your life.'

So the divil he hoisted her up on his back.
Right fol right fol tiddy fol lay;
So the divil he hoisted her up on his back.
And landed at hell's hall door with a crack.

There were two little divils a-playing with chains.
Right fol right fol tiddy fol lay;
There were two little divils a-playing with chains.
She upp'd with her stick and knocked out their brains.

There were two other devils looked over the wall.
Right fol right fol tiddy fol lay;
There were two other devils looked over the wall.
They said, 'Take her away or she'll murder us all.'

So the devil he hoisted her up on his back.
Right fol right fol tiddy fol lay;
So the devil he hoisted her up on his back.
And back to the old man hurried the pack.

They were seven years going, nine days coming back.
Right fol right fol tiddy fol lay;
They were seven years going, nine days coming back.
Yet she asked for the scrapings she left in the pot.

Says he, 'My good man, here's your wife safe and well.'
Right fol right fol tiddy fol lay;
Says he, 'My good man, here's your wife safe and well,
For she wouldn't be kept, not even in hell.'

'Now, I've been a divil the most of my life.'
Right fol right fol tiddy fol lay;
'Now, I've been a divil the most of my life,
But I ne'er was in hell tell I met with your wife.'

So it's true that the women are worse than the men,
Right fol right fol tiddy fol lay;
So it's true that the women are worse than the men,
For they went down to hell and were thrown our again.

Coortin' in the Kitchen

Anon

Come single belle and beau, to me now pay attention,
And love I'll plainly show is the devil's own invention.
For once in love I fell with a maiden so bewitching,
Miss Henrietta Bell down in Captain Phibbs's kitchen.

Chorus
Ri tooral ooral lah, ri tooral ooral addy;
Ri tooral ooral lah, ri tooral ooral addy.

At the age of seventeen I was tied unto a grocer,
Not far from Stephen's Green, where Miss Bell for tea would go, sir.
Her manners were so free, she set my heart a-twitching,
She invited me to tea down in Captain Phibbs's kitchen.

Next Sunday being the day, we were to have the flare-up,
I dressed myself quite gay an' I frizz'd an' oiled my hair up.
As the captain had no wife, he had gone out a-fishin';
So we kicked up high life below stairs in the kitchen.

Just as the clock struck six we sat down to the table;
She handed teas and cakes – I ate while I was able.
I ate cakes, drank punch and tea till my side had got a stitch in,
And the hours flew quick away, while coortin' in the kitchen.

With my arms around her waist I kissed – she hinted marriage –
To the door in dreadful haste came Captain Phibbs's carriage.
Her looks told me full well that moment she was wishin',
That I'd get out to h*** or somewhere far from the kitchen.

She flew up off my knees, full five feet up or higher,
And over head and heels threw me slap into the fire.
My new repealer's coat that I bought from Mr Stitchen,
With a thirty-shilling note went to blazes in the kitchen.

I grieved to see my duds all smeared with smoke and ashes,
When a tub of dirty suds right in my face she dashes.
As I lay on the floor still the water she kept pitchin',
Till the footman broke the door and marched down into the kitchen.

When the captain came downstairs though he seen my situation,
In spite of all my prayers I was marched off to the station.
For me they'd take no bail, tho' to get home I was itchin',
But I had to tell the tale of how I came into the kitchen.

I said she did invite me but she gave a flat denial.
For assault she did indict me and I was sent for trial.
She swore I robbed the house in spite of all her screechin',
And I got six months hard for my coortin' in the kitchen.

Lannigan's Ball

Anon

In the town of Athy, one Jeremy Lannigan,
Battered away till he hadn't a pound.
His father he died and made him a man again,
Left him a farm and ten acres of ground.
He gave a grand ball to his friends and relations,
Who did not forget him when sent to the wall.
If you'll only listen I'll make your eyes glisten,
At the rows and the ructions at Lannigan's ball.

Myself, to be sure, got free invitation,
For all the nice boys an' girls that I'd ask.
In less than a minute the friends and relations
Were dancing as merry as bees round a cask.
Miss O'Hara, the nice little milliner,
Tipp'd them a wink to give her a call,
And soon we arrived with Timothy Galligan,
Just in time for Lannigan's ball.

They were doing all sorts of nonsensical polkas,
All round the room in a neat whirligig,
But Julia and me soon banished such nonsense,
And tipped them a twist of a real Irish jig.
Och, mavrone, 'twas she that was glad o' me,
And danced till you'd think the ould ceiling would fall,
For I spent a whole fortnight at Burke's Academy,
Learnin' a step for Lannigan's ball.

The boys were all merry, the girls were all hearty,
Dancing away in couples and groups,
Till an accident happened young Terence McCarthy:
He put his leg on Miss Flaherty's hoops.
The creature she fainted, roared milia murder,
Called for her friends and gathered them all;
Ned Carmody swore that he'd go no further
But he'd have satisfaction at Lannigan's ball.

In the midst of the row Miss Kerrigan fainted,
Her cheeks all the while being as red as the rose.
Some of the ladies declared she was painted.
She took a small drop too much, I suppose.
Her sweetheart, Ned Morgan, so powerful and able,
When he saw his fair colleen stretched by the wall,
He tore a leg from under the table,
And smashed all the chaney at Lannigan's ball.

Oh, boys, there was a ruction;
Myself got a kick from big Phelim McHugh,
But soon I replied to this kind introduction,
And kicked up a terrible phillibooloo;
Ould Casey the piper was near being strangled;
They squeezed up his pipes, bellows, chanters and all;
The girls in their ribbons were all entangled
And that put an end to Lannigan's ball.

Finnegan's Wake

Anon

The Irishism in the last line comes from the imprecation: 'D'anam don diabhal' (lit. 'Your soul to the devil!').

Tim Finnegan lived in Walkin Street,
A gentleman Irish mighty odd.
He had a tongue both rich and sweet,
An' to rise in the world he carried a hod.
Now Tim had a sort of tipplin' way,
With the love of the liquor he was born
An' to help him on with his work each day,
He'd a drop of the craythur every morn.

Chorus
Whack fol the day, dance to your partner;
Welt the flure, yer trotters shake!
Wasn't it the truth I told you,
Lots of fun at Finnegan's wake.

One morning Tim was rather full;
His head felt heavy which mad him shake.
He fell from the ladder and broke his skull;
So they carried him home his corpse to wake.
They rolled him up in a nice clean sheet,
And laid him out upon the bed,
With a gallon of whiskey at his feet,
And a barrel of porter at his head.

His friends assembled at the wake,
And Mrs Finnegan called for lunch.
First they brought in tay and cake,
Then pipes, tobacco and whiskey punch.
Mrs Biddy O'Brien began to cry,
'Such a neat clean corpse, did you ever see?
Arrah, Tim, avourneen, why did you die?'
'Ah, hould yor gob,' said Paddy McGee.

Then Peggy O'Connor took up the job.
'Biddy,' says she, 'You're wrong, I'm sure.'
But Biddy gave her a belt on the gob,
And left her sprawling on the floor;
Oh then the war did soon engage:
'Twas woman to woman and man to man;
Shillelagh law was all the rage,
An' a row and a ruction soon began.

Then Mickey Maloney raised his head,
When a noggin of whiskey flew at him.
It missed and falling on the bed,
The liquor scattered over Tim;
Bedad he revives! See how he rises,
And Timothy rises from the bed,
Says, 'Whirl your liquor round like blazes;
Thanam on dhoul, do you think I'm dead?

Salonika

Anon

A Cork take on local participation in the British campaign against the Bulgarians around Salonika (now Thessalonika) during the First World War. Irish divisions fought in the area from 1915 to 1917

Oh me husband's in Salonika and I wonder if he's dead,
And I wonder if he knows he has a kid with a foxy head.

Chorus
So right away, so right away,
So right away Salonika, right away, me soldier boy.

When the war is over what will the slackers do?
They'll be all around the soldiers for the loan of a bob or two.

And when the war is over what will the soldiers do?
They'll be walking around with a leg and a half, and the slackers they'll
 have two.

And they taxed the pound of butter and the taxed the ha'penny bun,
And still with all their taxin' they can't bate the bloody Huns.

They taxed the Colosseum and they taxed St Mary's Hall.
Why don't they tax the Bobbies with their backs agin the wall.

When the war is over what will the slackers do?
For every kid in America, in Cork there will be two.

They takes us out to Blarney and they lays us on the grass,
They puts us in the family way and they leaves us on our arse.

There's lino in the parlour and in the kitchen too,
And there's a lovely glass back chiffonier we got from Dickie Drew.

Never marry a soldier, a sailor, or a marine,
But keep your eye on that Sinn Féin boy with his yellow, white and green.

from The Description of an Irish Feast

(from the Irish)
Jonathan Swift (1667-1745)

O'Rourk's noble feast,
Will ne'er be forgot,
By those who were there,
Or those who were not.

His revels to keep,
We sup and we dine,
On seven score sheep,
Fat bullocks and swine.

Usquebaugh to our feast,
In pails was brought up,
A hundred at least,
And a madder our cup.

O there is the sport!
We rise with the light,
In disorderly sort,
From snoring all night.

O how was I trick'd!
My pipe it was broke;
My pocket was pick'd;
I lost my new cloak.

I'm rifled, quoth Nell,
Of mantle and kercher:
Why then fare them well,
The de'el take the searcher.

Come harper, strike up;
But, first, by your favour,
Boy, give us a cup:
Ah! this hath some savour.

O'Rourk's jolly boys
Ne'er dreamt of the matter,
Till rous'd by the noise,
And musical clatter.

They bounce from their nest,
No longer will tarry,
They rise ready dressed,
Without one Ave-Mary.

They dance in a round,
Cutting capers and ramping;
A mercy the ground,
Did not burst with their stamping.

The floor is all wet
With leaps and with jumps,
While the water and sweat,
Splish-splash in their pumps.

Bring straw for our bed;
Shake it down to the feet,
Then over us spread,
The winnowing sheet.

Good Lord! what a sight,
After all their good cheer,
For people to fight,
In the midst of their beer!

They rise from their feast,
And hot are their brains;
A cubit at least,
The length of their skeans.

With cudgels of oak,
Well harden'd to flame,
A hundred heads broke,
A hundred struck lame.

Come down with that beam,
If cudgels are scarce,
A blow on the weam,
Or a kick on the arse.

The Friar of Orders Gray

John O'Keefe (1747–1833)

I am a friar of orders gray:
As down the valley I take my way,
I pull not blackberry, haw or hip,
Good store of venison does fill my scrip:
My long bead-roll I merrily chaunt,
Where'er I walk, no money I want;
And why I'm so plump the reason I'll tell –
Who leads a good life is sure to live well.
What baron or squire
Or knight of the shire
Lives half so well as a holy friar!

After supper, of heaven I dream,
But that is fat pullet and clouted cream.
Myself, by denial, I mortify,
With a dainty bit of a warden pie:
I'm clothed in sackcloth for my sin:
With old sack wine I'm lined within:
A chirping cup is my matin song,
And the vesper bell is my bowl's ding dong.
What baron or squire
Or knight of the shire
Lives half so well as a holy friar!

Let Us Be Merry before We Go

John Philpot Curran (1750–1817)

If sadly thinking, with spirits sinking,
Could, more than drinking, my cares compose,
A cure for sorrow from sighs I'd borrow,
And hope tomorrow would end my woes.
But as in wailing there's nought availing,
And death unfailing will strike the blow,
Then for that reason and for a season,
Let us be merry before we go.

To joy a stranger, a wayworn ranger,
In ev'ry danger my course I've run;
Now hope all ending and death befriending,
His last aid lending, my cares are done.
No more a rover or hapless lover,
My griefs are over – my glass runs low;
Then for that reason and for a season,
Let us be merry before we go.

Let the Toast Pass

Richard Brinsley Sheridan (1751–1816)

Here's to the maiden of bashful fifteen,
Here's to the widow of fifty;
Here's to the flaunting extravagant quean,
And here's to the housewife that's thrifty.

Chorus
Let the toast pass,
Drink to the lass,
I'll warrant she'll prove an excuse for the glass.

Here's to the charmer whose dimples we prize,
Now to the maid who has none, sir,
Here's to the girl with a pair of blue eyes,
And here's to the nymph with but one, sir!

Here's to the maid with a bosom of snow,
And to her that's as brown as a berry;
Here's to the wife with a face full of woe,
And now to the damsel that's merry:

For let 'em be clumsy or let 'em be slim,
Young or ancient, I care not a feather;
So fill the pint bumper quite up to the brim,
And let us e'en toast them together.

from The Night before Larry Was Stretched

Robert Burrows (1756–1841)

The night before Larry was stretched,
The boys they all paid him a visit.
A bait in their sacks too they fetched.
They sweated their duds till they riz it.
For Larry was ever the lad,
When a boy was condemned to the squeezer,
Would fence all the duds that he had,
To help a poor friend to a sneezer,
And warm his gob 'fore he died.

The boys they came crowding in fast;
They drew all their stools round about him.
Six glims round his trap-case were placed;
He couldn't be well waked without 'em.
When one of us asked could he die,
Without having duly repented,
Says Larry, 'That's all in my eye,
And first by the clergy invented
To get a fat bit for themselves.'

'I'm sorry, dear Larry!' says I,
'To see you in this situation;
And blister my limbs if I lie,
I'd as lief it had been my own station.'
'Ochone, it's all over,' says he,
'For the neckcloth I'll be forced to put on
And by this time tomorrow you'll see
Your poor Larry dead as a mutton.
And all 'cos my courage was good.

'And I'll be cut up like a pie
And my nob from my body be parted.'
'You're in the wrong box, then,' says I,
'For blast me if they're so hard-hearted;

A chalk on the back of your neck
Is all that Jack Ketch dares to give you;
Then mind not such trifles a feck,
For why should the likes of them grieve you?
And now, boys, come tip us the deck.'

The cards being called for they played,
Till Larry found one of them cheated.
A dart at his napper he made,
(The boy being easily heated);
'Oh by the hokey, you thief,
You cheat me because I'm in grief.
I'll scuttle your nob with my daddle!
But soon I'll demolish your noodle
And leave you your claret to drink.'

Then the clergy came in with his book.
He spoke him so smooth and so civil.
Larry tipped him a Kilmainham look,
And potched his big wig to the devil.
Then sighing he threw back his head
To get a sweet drop of the bottle,
And pitiful sighing he said,
'O the hemp will be soon round the throttle,
And choke my poor windpipe to death.'

'Though sure it's the best way to die,
O the devil a better a-livin'!
For when the gallows is high,
Your journey is shorter to heaven;
But what harasses Larry the most,
And makes his poor soul melancholy,
Is that he thinks of the time when his ghost
Will come in a sheet to sweet Molly.
O sure it will kill her alive.'

So moving these last words he spoke,
We all vented our tears in a shower.
For my part, I thought my heart broke,
To see him cut down like a flower.
On his travels we watched him next day.
O the throttler, I thought I could kill him;
But Larry not one word did say,
Nor changed till he come to 'King William'.
Then, musha, his colour grew white.

When he came to the numbing chit,
He was tucked up so neat and so pretty.
The rumbler jogged off his feet,
And he died with his feet to the city.
He kicked **too** – but that was all pride.
For soon you might see 'twas all over.
Soon after the noose was untied
And at darkee we waked him in clover
And sent him to take a ground sweat.

The Finding of Moses

'Zozimus' (Michael Moran) (1794–1846)

On Egypt's banks, contagious to the Nile,
The ould Pharaoh's daughter, she went to bathe in style.
She took her dip and she came unto the land,
And to dry her royal pelt she ran along the strand.
A bulrush tripped her, whereupon she saw,
A smiling baby in a wad of straw;
She took him up and says she in accents mild,
'Oh, taranagers, girls, now which of yis owns the child?'

She took him up and she gave a little grin,
For she and Moses were standing in their skin.
'Bedad, now,' says she, 'It was someone very rude,
Left a little baby by the river in his nude.'
She took him to her ould lad sitting on the throne.
'Da,' says she, 'Will you give the boy a home?'
'Bedad, now,' says he. 'Sure I've often brought in worse.
Go, my darlin' daughter, and get the child a nurse.'

An oul' blackamore woman among the crew
Cried out, 'You royal savage, what's that to do with you?
Your royal ladies is too meek and mild,
To beget dishonestly this darling little child.'
'Ah then,' says Pharaoh, 'I'll search every nook,
From the Phoenix Park down to Donnybrook,
And when I catch hoult of the bastard's father,
I will kick him from the Nile down to the Dodder.'

Well they sent a bellman to the Market Square,
To see if they could find a slavey there,
But the only one now that he could find,
Was the little one that left the child behind.
She came up to Pharaoh, a stranger, mor-yah,
Never lettin' on that she was the baby's ma.
And so little Moses got his mammy back,
Shows that co-in-ci-dence is a nut to crack.

The Woman of Three Cows

James Clarence Mangan (1804–49)

(from the Irish)

O Woman of Three Cows, agra, don't let your tongue thus rattle!
Oh don't be saucy, don't be stiff, because you may have cattle,
I have seen – and here's my hand to you. I only say what's true –
A many a one has twice your stock not half as proud as you.

Good luck to you, don't scorn the poor and don't be their despiser;
For worldly wealth soon melts away and cheats the very miser;
And death soon strips the wealth from haughty human brows,
The don't be stiff and don't be proud, good Woman of Three Cows.

See where Momonia's heroes lie, proud Owen Mór's descendants,
'Tis they that won the glorious name and had the grand attendants;
If they are forced to bow to fate, as every mortal bows,
Can you be proud, can you be stiff, my Woman of Three Cows?

The brave sons of Lord Clare, they left the land to mourning,
Mavrone! For they were banished, with no hope of their returning.
Who knows in what abode of want those youths were driven to house?
Yet you can give yourself these airs, O Woman of Three Cows.

O, think of Donnell of the Ships, the chief whom nothing daunted,
See how he fell in distant Spain unchronicled, unchanted!
He sleeps, the great O'Sullivan, where thunder cannot rouse –
Then ask yourself, should you be proud, good Woman of Three Cows?

O'Ruark, Maguire, those souls of fire, whose names are shrined in story:
Think how heir high achievements once made Erin's glory.
Yet now their bones lie mouldering under weeds and cypress boughs, –
And so, for all your pride, will yours, O Woman of Three Cows.

Th' O'Carrolls, also, famed when fame was only for the boldest,
Rest in forgotten sepulchres with Erin's best and oldest;
Yet who so great as they of yore in battle or carouse?
Just think of that and hide your head, good Woman of Three Cows.

Your neighbour's poor; and you, it seems, are big with vain ideas,
Because, for sooth, you've got three cows – one more, I see, than she has;
That tongue of yours wags more at times than charity allows,
But if you're strong, be merciful, great Woman of Three Cows.

Avran (Song)
Now, there you go; you still keep up your scornful bearing,
And I'm too poor to hinder you; but by the cloak I'm wearing,
If I had but four cows myself, even though you were my spouse,
I'd thwack you well, to cure your pride, my Woman of Three Cows.

Widow Malone

Charles Lever (1805–72)

Did you hear of the Widow Malone,
    Ohone!
Who lived in the town of Athlone?
    Ohone!
Oh, she melted the hearts,
Of the swains in them parts,
So lovely the Widow Malone,
    Ohone!
So lovely the Widow Malone.

Of lovers she had a full score,
    Or more
And fortunes they all had galore,
    In store.
From the minister down,
To the clerk of the crown,
All were courting the Widow Malone,
    Ohone!
All were courting the Widow Malone.

But so modest was Widow Malone,
    'Twas known,
That no one could see her alone,
    Ohone!
Let them ogle and sigh,
They could ne'er catch her eye,
So bashful the Widow Malone,
    Ohone
So bashful the Widow Malone,

Till one Mister O'Brien from Clare,
    How quare!
It's little for blushing they care,
    Down there.
Put his arm round her waist–

Gave ten kisses at laste –
'Oh,' says he, 'you're my Molly Malone,
　　My own!'
'Oh,' says he, 'you're my Molly Malone.

And the widow they all thought so shy,
　　My eye!
Ne'er thought of a simper or sigh,
　　For why?
But 'Lucius,' says she,
'Since you've now made so free,
You may marry your Molly Malone,
　　Ohone,
You may marry your Molly Malone.'

There's a moral contained in my song,
　　Not wrong,
And one comfort, it's not very long,
　　But strong,
If for widows you die,
Learn to kiss, not to sigh,
For they're all like sweet Mistress Malone,
　　Ohone!
For they're all like sweet Mistress Malone.

from Peg of Limavaddy

William Makepeace Thackeray (1811–63)

Riding from Coleraine
    (Famed for lovely Kitty),
Came a Cockney bound
    On to Derry City,
Weary was his soul.
    Shivering and sad he,
Bumped along the road,
    Leads to Limavaddy.

...

Limavaddy's inn's,
    But a humble baithouse,
Where you may procure,
    Whiskey and potatoes;
Landlord at the door,
    Gives a smiling welcome,
To the shivering wights,
    Who to his hotel come,
Landlady within,
    Sits and knits a stocking,
With a wary foot
    Baby's cradle rocking.

...

Presently a maid,
    Enters with the liquor,
(Half a pint of ale,
    Frothing in a beaker.)
Gods! I didn't know,
    What my beating heart meant.
Hebe's self I thought,
    Enter'd the apartment.
As she came she smiled,

And the smile bewitching,
 On my word and honour,
Lighted all the kitchen!

With a curtsey neat,
 Greeting the newcomer,
Lovely smiling Peg,
 Offers me the rummer.
But my trembling hand,
 Up the beaker tilted,
And the glass of ale,
 Every drop I spilt it.
Spilt it every drop,
 (Dames who read my volumes
Pardon such a word.)
 On my what d'ye call 'ems!

Witnessing the sight,
 Of that dire disaster,
Out began to laugh,
 Miss, maid and master;
Such a merry peal,
 'Specially Miss Peg's was,
(As the glass of ale,
 Trickling down my legs was).
That the joyful sound,
 Of that ringing laughter,
Echoed in my ears,
 Many a long day after.

...

When the laugh was done,
 Peg, the pretty hussy,
Moved about the room,
 Wonderfully busy;
Now she looks to see,
 If the kettle keep hot,
Now she rubs the spoons,

Now she cleans the teapot;
Now she sets the cups,
    Trimly and secure,
Now she scours the pot,
    And so it was I drew her.

...

This I do declare:
    Happy is the laddy,
Who the heart can share,
    Of Peg of Limavaddy;
Married if she were,
    Blest would be the daddy,
Of the children fair,
    Of Peg of Limavaddy;
Beauty is not rare,
    In the land of Paddy;
Fair beyond compare,
    Is Peg of Limavaddy.

Irish Annals

William Allingham (1824–89)

A response to John O'Donovan's translation of the Annals of the Four Masters *in 1856*

MacMurlagh kill'd Flantagh, and Cormac Killed Hugh,
Having else no particular business to do.
O'Toole killed O'Gorman, O'More killed O'Leary,
Muldearg, son of Phadrig, killed Con, son of Cleary.
Three show'rs in the reign of King Niall the Good,
Rain'd silver and honey and smoking red blood.

Saint Colman converted a number of pagans,
And got for his friars some land of O'Hagan's;
The king and his clansmen rejoiced at this teaching,
And paused from their fighting to come to the preaching.
The Abbot of Gort, with good reason, no doubt,
With the Abbot of Ballinamallard fell out,
Set fire to the abbey-roof over his head,
And kill'd a few score of his monks, the rest fled.

The Danes, furious pirates by water and dry-land.
Put boats on Lough Erne and took Devenish Island;
The monks being used to such things, in a trice
Snatching relics and psalters and vessels of price,
Got into the round tower and pull'd up the ladder;
Their end, for the Danes lit a fire, was the sadder.

Young Donnell slew Rory, then Dermod slew Connell;
O'Lurcan of Cashel kill'd Phelim his cousin,
On family matters. Some two or three dozen,
Of this tribe, in consequence, killed one another.
MacFogarty put out the eyes of his brother,
James Longthair, lest James should be chosen for chief.
At Candlemas, fruit trees this year were in leaf.

King Toole, an excitable man in his cups,
Falls out with King Rorke about two deerhounds pups
And scouring the north, without risking a battle,
Burns down all the houses, drives off all the cattle,
King Rorke to invade the south country arouses,
Drives off all the cattle, burns down all the houses.
If you wish for more slaughters and crimes and disasters
See, passim, those annalists called 'The Four Masters'.

Father O'Flynn

Alfred Perceval Graves (1846–1931)

Of priests we can offer a charmin' variety,
Far renowned for larnin' and piety.
Still I'd advance ye widout impropriety,
    Father O'Flynn as the flower of them all.

Chorus
Here's a health you, Father O'Flynn,
Sláinte and sláinte and sláinte agin;
Powerfulest preacher and
Tinderest teacher and
Kindliest creature in ould Donegal.

Don't talk of your Provost and Fellows of Trinity,
Famous for ever at Greek and Latinity,
Faix and the divels and all at divinity
    Father O'Flynn'd make hares of them all.

Come, I vinture to give ye my word,
Never the likes of his logic was heard,
Down from mythology into thayology,
    Troth! and conchology if he'd the call.

Och! Father O'Flynn, you've the wonderful way wid you.
All the ould sinners are wishful to pray wid you.
All the young childer are wild for to play with you.
    You've such a way wid you, Father avick!

Still for all you've so gentle a soul,
Gad, you've your flock in your grandest control,
Checking the crazy ones,
Coaxin' onaisy ones,
Liftin' the lazy ones on wid the stick.

And though quite avoidin' all foolish frivolity,
Still at all seasons of innocent jollity,

Where was the playboy could claim an equality
    At comicality, Father, wid you?

Once the bishop looked grave at your jest,
Till this remark set him off with rest:
'Is it lave gaiety all to the laity?
Cannot the clergy be Irishmen too?'

Abdul Abulbul Ameer

Percy French (1854–1920)

The sons of the Prophet are brave men and bold,
And quite unaccustomed to fear,
But the bravest by far in the ranks of the Shah,
Was Abdul Abulbul Ameer.
If you wanted a man to encourage the van,
Or shout 'Attaboy' in the rear,
Or storm a redoubt, you had only to shout,
For Abdul Abulbul Ameer.

Now the heroes were many and well known to fame,
In the troops that were led by the Tsar,
But the bravest of these, whom no man could appease,
Was Ivan Skivinsky Skivar.
He could imitate Irving, play poker and pool,
And perform on the Spanish guitar.
In fact, quite the cream of the Muscovite team,
Was Ivan Skivinsky Skivar.

One day this bold Russian, he shouldered his gun,
And donned his most cynical sneer.
Down town he did go, where he trod on the toe,
Of Abdul Abulbul Ameer.
'Young man,' quoth Abdul, 'Has your life grown so dull,
That you wish to end your career?
Vile infidel, know, you have trod on the toe,
Of Abdul Abulbul Ameer.'

Said Ivan, 'My friend, your remarks in the end,
Will avail you but little, I fear,
For you'll never survive to repeat them alive,
Mr Abdul Abulbul Ameer.'
'The take your last look on sunshine and brook,
And send your regrets to the Tsar,
By this I imply, you are going to die,
Count Ivan Skivinsky Skivar.'

Then the bold Mameluke drew his trusty skibouk,
With a cry of 'Allah Ak-Bar'.
And with deadly intent he ferociously went,
For Ivan Skivinsky Skivar.
They fought through the night in the pale yellow light;
The din it was heard from afar,
And huge multitudes came, so immense was the fame,
Of Abdul and Ivan Skivar.

As Abdul's long knife was extracting the life,
(In fact he was shouting, 'Huzza!')
He felt himself struck by that wily Calmuck,
Count Ivan Skivinsky Skivar.
The Sultan drove by in his red-breasted fly,
Expecting the victor to cheer,
But he only drew near to hear the last sigh,
Of Abdul Abulbul Ameer.

Tsar Petrovitch, too, in his spectacles blue,
Drove up in his new-crested car.
He arrived just in time to exchange a last line,
With Ivan Skivinsky Skivar.
A tombstone arose where the blue Danube flows,
And graved there in characters clear,
Are: 'Stranger, pass by but contribute a sigh,
For Abdul Abulbul Ameer.

A Muscovite maiden her lone vigil keeps,
'Neath the light of the pale polar star,
And the name that she murmurs so oft as she weeps,
Is Ivan Skivinsky Skivar.

Phil the Fluter's Ball

Percy French (1854–1920)

Have you heard of Phil the Fluter, of the town of Ballymuck?
The times were going hard with him in fact the man was broke.
So he just sent out a notice to his neighbours, one and all,
As to how he'd like their company that evening at a ball.
And when writin' out he was careful to suggest to them,
That if they found a hat of his convanient to the dure,
The more they put in whenever he requested them,
The better would the music be for battherin' the flure.

Chorus
With the toot of the flute,
And the twiddle of the fiddle, O;
Hopping in the middle, like a herrin' on the griddle, O,
Up! down, hands aroun',
Crossing to the wall.
Oh! hadn't we the gaiety at Phil the Fluter's ball.

There was Misther Denis Dogherty, who kep' the runnin' dog;
There was little crooked Paddy from the Tiraloughett bog;
There was boys from every barony and girls from ev'ry 'art',
And the beautiful Miss Bradys in a private ass and cart,
And along with them came bouncing Mrs Cafferty;
Little Micky Mulligan was also to the fore,
Rose, Suzanne and Margaret O'Rafferty,
The flower of Ardmagullion and the pride of Pethravore.

First, little Micky Mulligan got up to show them how,
And then the Widda Cafferty steps out and makes her bow.
'I could dance you off your legs,' sez she, 'as sure as you are born,
If ye'll only make the piper play "The Hare Was in the Corn".'
So Phil plays up to the best of his ability;
The lady and the gentleman began to do their share;
'Faith. then, Mick, it's you that has ability.'
'Begorra, Mrs Cafferty, yer leppin' like a hare!'

Then Phil the Fluter tipped a wink to little crooked Pat.
'I think it's nearly time,' sez he, 'for passin' round the hat.'
So Paddy passed the caubeen round and looking mighty cute,
Sez, 'You have to pay the piper when he tootles on the flute.'
Then all joined in with the greatest joviality,
Covering the 'buckle', the 'shuffle' and the 'cut';
Jigs were danced, of the very finest quality
But the Widda bet the company at handlin' the fut.

Slattery's Mounted Foot

Percy French (1854–1920)

You've heard o' Julius Caesar an' the great Napoleon, too,
An' how the Cork Militia beat the Turks at Waterloo,
But there's a page of glory that a yet remains uncut,
An' that's the martial story o' the Shlathery Mounted Fut.
This gallant corps was organised by Shlathery's eldest son,
A single-minded poacher, wid a double-breasted gun;
An' many a head was opened, aye, an many an eye was shut,
Whin practisin' manoeuvres in the Shlathery's Mounted Fut.

Chorus
An' down from the mountains came the squadrons an' platoons,
Four-an'-twinty fightin' min, an' a couple o' sthout gossoons,
An' whin we marched behind the dhrum to patriotic tunes.
We felt that fame would gild the name o' Shlathery's Light Dragoons.

Well, first we reconnoithered round O'Sullivan's shebeen;
It used to be 'The Shop House' but we called it 'The Canteen'.
But there we saw a notice which the bravest heart unnerved:
'All liquor must be settled for before the dhrink is served.'
So on we marched, but soon again each warrior's heart grew pale,
For rising up in front o' us we saw the County Jail;
And when the army faced about, 'twas just in time to find,
A couple o' stout policemin had surrounded us behind.

Chorus
Still down from the mountains came the squadrons an' platoons,
Four-an'-twinty fightin' min, an' a couple o' sthout gossoons,
Says Shlathery, 'We must circumvent these bludgeonin' bosthoons,
Or else it sames they'll take the names o' Shlathery's Light Dragoons.

'We'll cross the ditch,' our leader cried, 'an' take the foe in flank,'
But yells of consternation here arose from every rank,
For posted high upon a tree we very plainly saw,
'Trespassers prosecuted in accordance wid the law.'

'We're foiled!' exclaimed bould Shlathery, 'Here ends our grand
    campaign.
'Tis merely throwin' life away to face that mearin' drain.
I'm not as bold as lions but I'm braver nor a hin,
An' he that fights and runs away will live to fight again.'

Chorus
And back to the mountains went the squadrons an' platoons,
Four-an'-twinty fightin' min, an' a couple o' sthout gossoons,
The band was playing cautiously their patriotic tunes,
To sing the fame, if rather lame, o' Shlathery's Light Dragoons.

The Curse

J.M. Synge (1871–1909)

To a sister of an enemy of the author's who disapproved of The Playboy

Lord, confound this surly sister,
Blight her brow with blotch and blister,
Cramp her larynx, lung and liver,
In her guts a galling give her.
Let her live to earn her dinners,
In Mountjoy with seedy sinners;
Lord, this judgment quickly bring,
And I'm your servant, J. M. Synge.

The Gap o' Dreams

St Patrick's Breastplate

Anon

I bind unto myself today,
The strong name of the Trinity,
By invocation of the same,
The Three in One and One in Three.

I bind this day to me forever,
By power of faith, Christ's incarnation;
His baptism in the Jordan river;
His death on the Cross for my salvation;
His bursting from the spiced tomb;
His riding up the heavenly way;
His coming at the day of doom;

I bind unto myself today,
The virtues of the starlit heaven,
The glorious sun's lifegiving ray,
The whiteness of the moon at even,
The flash of the lightning free,
The whirling wind's tempestuous shocks,
The stable earth, the deep salt sea
Around the old eternal rocks.

I bind unto myself today,
The power of God to hold and lead,
His eye to watch, his might to stay,
His ear to hearken to my need,
The wisdom of my God to teach,
His hand to guide, His shield to ward,
The word of God to give me speech,
His heavenly body to be my guard.

Christ be with me, Christ within me,
Christ behind me, Christ before me,
Christ beside me, Christ to win me,
Christ to comfort and restore me,

Christ beneath me, Christ above me,
Christ in quiet, Christ in danger,
Christ in hearts of all that love me,
Christ in mouth of friend and stranger.

I bind unto myself today the Name,
The strong Name of the Trinity;
By invocation of the same,
The Three in One and One in Three,
Of whom all nature hath creation,
Eternal Father, Spirit, Word,
Praise to the Lord of my salvation:
Salvation is of Christ the Lord.

Columcille the Scribe

Translation by Kuno Meyer (1859–1919)

My hand is weary with writing;
My sharp quill is not steady.
My slender-beaked pen pours forth,
A black draught of shining dark-blue ink.

A stream of the wisdom of blessed God,
Springs from my fair brown shapely hand:
On the page it squirts its draught,
Of ink of the green-skinned holly.

My little dripping pen travels,
Across the plain of shining books,
Without ceasing for the wealth of the great –
Whence my hand is weary with writing.

While Shepherds Watched

Nahum Tate (1652– 1715)

While shepherds watched their flocks by night,
All seated on the ground,
The angel of the Lord came down,
And glory shone around.
'Fear not,' said he, for mighty dread
Had seized their troubled mind;
'Glad tidings of great joy I bring
To you and all mankind.'

'To you in David's town this day
Is born of David's line,
The saviour who is Christ the Lord
And this shall be the sign:
The heavenly babe you there shall find,
To human view displayed,
All meanly wrapped in swaddling bands,
And in a manger laid.'

Thus spake the seraph and forthwith,
Appeared a shining throng,
Of angels praising God, who thus,
Addressed their joyful song:
'All glory be to God on high,
And to the earth be peace;
Goodwill henceforth from heaven to men
Begin and never cease.'

I Saw from the Beach

Thomas Moore (1779–1852)

I saw from the beach, when the morning was shining,
A bark o'er the waters move gloriously on.
I came when the sun o'er that beach was declining,
The bark was still there, but the waters were gone!

And such is the fate of life's early promise,
So passing the springtide of joy we have known.
Each wave that we danc'd on at morning, ebbs from us,
And leaves us, at eve, on the bleak shore alone!

Ne'er tell me of glories serenely adorning.
The close of our day, the calm eve of our night.
Give me back, give me back the wild freshness of morning,
Her clouds and her tears are worth evening's best light.

Oh, who would not welcome that moment's returning,
When passion first wak'd a new life through his frame.
And his soul, like the wood that grows precious in burning,
Gave out all its sweets to love's exquisite flame!

The Song of Fionnuala

Thomas Moore (1779–1852)

Silent, O Moyle, be the roar of thy water,
Break not, ye breezes, your chain of repose,
While, murmuring mournfully, Lir's lonely daughter
Tells to the night-star her tale of woes.
When shall the swan her death-note singing,
Sleep, with wings in darkness furled?
When will Heaven, its sweet bell ringing,
Call my spirit from this stormy world?

Sadly, O Moyle, to thy winter-wave weeping,
Fate bids me languish long ages away;
Yet still in her darkness doth Erin lie sleeping,
Still doth the pure light its dawning delay.
When will that day-star, mildly springing,
Warm our isle with peace and love?
When will Heaven, its sweet bell ringing,
Call my spirit to the fields above?

The Enchanted Island

Luke Aylmer Connolly (c. 1786–1833)

To Rathlin's Isle I chanced to sail,
When summer breezes softly blew,
And there I heard so sweet a tale,
That oft I wished it could be true.

They said, at eve, when rude winds sleep,
And hushed is ev'ry turbid swell,
A mermaid rises from the deep,
And sweetly tunes her magic shell.

And when she plays, rock, dell and cave,
In dying falls the sound retain,
As if some choral spirit gave,
Their aid to swell her witching strain.

Then summoned by that dulcet note,
Uprising to th' admiring view,
A fairy island seemed to float,
With tints of many a gorgeous hue.

And glittering fanes and lofty towers,
All on this fairy isle are seen;
And waving trees and shady bowers,
With more than mortal verdure green.

And as it moves, the western sky,
Glows with a thousand varying rays;
And the calm sea, tinged with each dye,
Seems like a golden flood of haze.

They also say, if earth or stone,
From verdant Erin's hallowed land,
Were on this magic island thrown,
For ever fixed it then would stand.

But when for this some little boat,
In silence ventures from the shore,
The mermaid sinks – hushed is the note –
The fairy isle is seen no more.

The Burial of Sir John Moore

Charles Wolfe (1791–1823)

The hero is Sir John Moore who commanded the British forces in Portugal and was killed at the Battle of Corunna on 18 January 1809.

Not a drum was heard, not a funeral note,
As his corse to the ramparts we hurried;
Not a soldier discharged his farewell shot,
O'er the grave where our hero we buried.

We buried him darkly, at dead of night,
The sods with our bayonets turning,
By the struggling moonbeam's misty light,
And the lantern dimly burning.

No useless coffin enclosed his breast;
Not in sheet nor in shroud we wound him;
But he lay like a warrior taking his rest,
With his martial cloak around him.

Few and short were the prayers we said,
And we spake not a word of sorrow,
But we steadfastly gazed on the face that was dead,
And we bitterly thought of the morrow.

We though as we hollowed his narrow bed,
And smoothed down his lonely pillow,
That the foe and the stranger would tread o'er his head,
And we far away on the billow!

Lightly they'll talk of the spirit that's gone,
And o'er his cold ashes upbraid him,
But little he'll reck if they let him sleep on,
In a grave where a Briton has laid him.

But half of our heavy task was done,
When the clock struck the hour for retiring,
And we heard the distant and random gun,
That the foe was sullenly firing.

Slowly and sadly we laid him down,
From the field of his fame fresh and gory;
We carved not a line and we raised not a stone –
But we left him alone in his glory!

Hy-Brasail – The Isle of the Blest

Gerald Griffin (1803-40)

On the ocean that hollows the rocks where ye dwell,
A shadowy land has appeared, as they tell.
Men thought it a region of sunshine and rest,
And they called it Hy-Brasail, the isle of the blest.

From year unto year on the ocean's blue rim,
The beautiful spectre showed lovely and dim.
The golden clouds curtained the deep where it lay,
And it looked like an Eden, away, far away!

A peasant who heard of the wonderful tale,
In the breeze of the Orient loosened his sail.
From Ara, the holy, he turned to the west,
For though Ara was holy, Hy-Brasail was blest.

He heard not the voices that called from the shore –
He heard not the rising wind's menacing roar.
Home, kindred and safety he left on that day,
And he sped to Hy-Brasail, away, far away!

Morn rose on the deep and that shadowy isle,
O'er the faint rim of distance reflected its smile.
Noon blazed on the waves and that shadowy shore,
Seemed lovelily distant and faint as before.

Lone evening came down on the wanderer's track
And to Ara again he looked timidly back.
Oh, far on the verge of the ocean it lay;
Yet the isle of the blest was away, far away!

Rash dreamer, return! O, ye winds of the main,
Bear him back to his own peaceful Ara again.
Rash fool! for a vision of fanciful bliss,
To barter they calm life of labour and peace.

The warning of reason was spoken in vain.
He never visited Ara again!
Night fell on the deep, amidst tempest and spray
And he died on the waters, away, far away!

All Things Bright and Beautiful

Cecil Frances Alexander (1818–95)

All things bright and beautiful,
All creatures great and small,
All things wise and wonderful –
The Lord God made them all.

Each little flower that opens,
Each little bird that sings –
He made their glowing colour,
He made their tiny wings.

The purple-headed mountain,
The river running by,
The sunset and the morning –
That brightens up the sky;

The cold wind in the winter,
The pleasant summer sun,
The ripe fruits in the garden –
He made them every one.

He gave us eyes to see them,
And lips that we might tell,
How great is God Almighty –
Who has made all things well.

Once in Royal David's City

Cecil Frances Alexander (1818–95)

Once in Royal David's City,
Stood a lonely cattle shed,
Where a mother laid her baby,
In a manger for his bed;
Mary was that mother mild,
Jesus Christ her little child.

He came down to earth from heaven,
Who is God and lord of all,
And his shelter was a stable,
And his cradle was a stall.
With the poor and mean and lowly,
Lived on earth our saviour holy.

And through all his wondrous childhood,
He would honour and obey,
Love and watch the lowly maiden,
In whose gentle arms he lay.
Christian children all must be,
Mild, obedient, good as he.

from The Legend of Stumpie's Brae

Cecil Frances Alexander (1818–95)

Heard ye no' tell of the Stumpie's Brae?
    Sit down, sit down, young friend.
I'll make your flesh to creep today,
    And your hair to stan' on end.

I mind it weel, in my younger days,
    The story yet was rife:
There dwelt within that lonely place,
    A farmer man and his wife.

The boys and girls were gone down all,
    A wee to the blacksmith's wake;
There pass'd ane on by the window small,
    And guv the door a shake.

The man he up and open'd the door
    When he had spoken a bit,
A pedlar man stepp'd into the floor.
Down he tumbled the pack he bore; right heavy pack was it.

'Gude save us a',' ays the wife, wi' a smile,
    'But yours is a thrivin' trade.'
'Ay, ay, I've wander'd mony a mile,
    And plenty have I made.'

The man sat on by the dull fire frame,
    When the pedlar went to rest;
Close to his ear the devil came,
    And slipp'd intil his breast.

He loo'd at his wife by the dim fire light
    And she was as bad as he –
'Could we no' murder thon man the night?'
    'Ay, could we, ready,' quo' she.

He took the pickaxe without a word,
    Whence it stood, ahint the door;
As he pass'd in, the sleeper stirr'd,
    That never wakened more.

'He's dead!' says the auld man, coming back –
    'What o' the corp, my dear?'
'We'll bury him snug in his ain bit pack,
Never ye mind for the loss of the sack,
    I've ta'en out a' the gear.'

'The pack's owre short by twa gude span.
    What'll we do?' quo' he –
'Oh, you're a doited, unthoughtfu' man.
    'We'll cut him off at the knee.'

They shovelled a hole right speedily;
    They laid him on his back –
'A right pair are ye,' quo' the pedlar, quo' he,
    Sitting bolt upright in the pack.

'Ye think ye've laid me snugly here
    And none shall know my station
But I'll hant ye far and I'll hant ye near,
Father and son, wi' terror and fear, to the nineteenth generation.'

It had stricken nine, just nine o' the clock –
    The hour when the man lay dead;
There came to the outer door a knock,
    And a heavy, heavy tread.

The old man's head swam round and round.
    The woman's blood 'gan freeze,
For it was not like a natural sound
But like some one stumping o'er the ground on the banes of his twa bare
    knees.

And through the door, like a sough of air,
    And stump, stump, round the twa,

Wi' his bloody head, and his knee banes bare –
    They'd maist ha'e died of awe!

The wife's black locks ere morn grew white,
    They say, as the mountain snaws;
The man was as straight as a staff that night,
    But he stoop'd when the morning rose.

Still, year and day, as the clock struck nine,
    The hour when they did the sin.
The wee bit dog began to whine,
    And the ghaist came clatterin' in.

Ae night there was a fearful flood –
    Three days the skies had poured,
And white wi' foam and black wi' mud,
    The burn in fury roar'd.

Quo' she, 'Gud man, ye need na turn,
    Say pale in the dim fire light;
The Stumpie canna cross the burn,
    He'll no' be here the night.

'For it's o'er the bank and it's o'er the linn,
    And it's up to the meadow ridge –'
'Ay,' quo' the Stumpie, hirpling in
And he gied the wife a slap on the chin, 'But I cam' round by the bridge!'

They sold their gear and over the sea,
    To a foreign land they went.
Over the sea – but wha can flee,
    His appointed punishment?

In the woods of wild America,
    Their weary feet they set.
But Stumpie was there the first, they say,
And he haunted them on to their dying day and he follows their
    children yet.

The Fairies

William Allingham (1824–89)

Up the airy mountain,
Down the rushy glen,
We daren't go a-hunting,
For fear of little men;
Wee folk, good folk,
Trooping all together;
Green jacket, redcap,
And white owl's feather!

Down along the rocky shore,
Some make their home.
They live on crispy pancakes,
Of yellow tide foam,
Some in the reeds,
Of the black mountain lake,
With frogs for their watchdogs,
All night awake.

High on the hilltop,
The old king sits.
He is now so old and grey,
He's nigh lost his wits.
With a bridge of white mist,
Columbkill he crosses,
On his stately journeys,
From Slievleague to Rosses;

Or going up with music,
On cold starry nights,
To sup with the queen
Of the gay Northern Lights,
They stole little Bridget,
For seven years long.
When she came down again,
Her friends were all gone.

They took her lightly back,
Between the night and morrow.
They thought that she was fast asleep,
But she was dead with sorrow.
They have kept her ever since,
Deep within the lake,
On a bed of flag-leaves,
Watching till she wake.

By the craggy hillside,
Through the mosses bare,
They have planted thorn-trees,
For pleasure here and there.
Is any man so daring,
As dig them up in spite,
He shall find their sharpest thorns,
In his bed at night.

Up the airy mountain,
Down the rushy glen,
We daren't go a-hunting,
For fear of little men;
Wee folk, good folk
Trooping all together;
Green jacket, redcap,
And white owl's feather!

The Leprahaun

Robert Dwyer Joyce (1830–83)

In a shady nook one moonlit night,
A leprahaun I spied,
In scarlet cap and coat of green,
A cruiskeen by his side.
'Twas tick-tack-tick, his hammer went,
Upon a weeny shoe,
And I laughed to think of a purse of gold,
But the fairy was laughing too.

With tiptoe step and beating heart,
Quite softly I drew nigh.
There was mischief in his merry face,
A twinkle in his eye;
He hammered and sang with tiny voice,
And sipped his mountain dew;
Oh! I laughed to think he was caught at last,
But the fairy was laughing too.

As quick as thought I grasped the elf,
'Your fairy purse,' I cried.
'My purse?' said he, ''tis in her hand,
That lady by your side.'
I turned to look; the elf was off,
And what was I to do?
Oh! I laughed to think what a fool I'd been,
And the fairy was laughing too.

Ode

Arthur O'Shaughnessy (1844–81)

We are the music-makers
And we are the dreamers of dreams,
Wandering by lone sea-breakers
And sitting by desolate streams,
World-losers and word-forsakers
On whom the pale moon gleams.
Yet we are the movers and shakers
Of the world for ever, it seems.

With wonderful deathless ditties
We build up the world's great cities,
And out of the fabulous story
We fashion an empire's glory.
One man with a dream, at pleasure
Shall go forth and conquer a crown,
And three with a new song's measure
Can trample an empire down.

We, in the ages lying
In the buried past of the earth,
Built Nineveh with our sighing
And Babel itself with our mirth.
And o'erthrew them with prophesying
To the old of the new world's worth.
For each is an age that is dying
Or one that is coming to birth.

Danny Boy

Fred E. Weatherly (1848–1929)

O Danny Boy, the pipes, the pipes are calling,
From glen to glen and down the mountain side;
The summer's gone and all the roses falling;
It's you, it's you must go and I must bide.

But come ye back when summer's in the meadow,
Or when the valley's hushed and white with snow;
It's I'll be here in sunshine or in shadow,
O Danny Boy, O Danny Boy, I love you so.

But when ye come, and all the flowers are dying,
And I am dead, as dead I well may be,
Ye'll come and find the place where I am lying,
And kneel and say an Ave there for me.

And I shall hear though soft ye tread above me,
And all my grave will warmer, sweeter be,
For you will bend and tell me that you love me,
And I shall sleep in peace until you come to me.

The Dead at Clonmacnoise

(from the Irish)
T.W. Rolleston (1857–1920)

In a quiet water'd land, a land of roses,
Stands Saint Kieran's city fair,
And the warriors of Erin in their famous generation,
Slumber there.

There beneath the dewy hillside sleep the noblest,
Of the clan of Conn.
Each below his stone with name in branching Ogham,
And the sacred knot thereon.

There they laid to rest the seven Kings of Tara;
There the sons of Cairbré sleep –
Battle-banners of the Gael, that in Kieran's plain of crosses,
Now their final hosting keep.

And in Clonmacnoise they laid the men of Teffia,
And right many a lord of Breagh,
Deep the sod above Clan Creidé and Clan Conaill,
Kind in hall and fierce in fray.

Many and many a son of Conn, the Hundred-Fighter,
In the red earth lies at rest;
Many a blue eye of Clan Colman the turf covers,
Many a swan-white breast.

The Fairies' Lullaby from the Gaelic

Eleanor Hull (1860–1935)

My mirth and merriment, soft and sweet art thou,
Child of the race of Conn art thou,
My mirth and merriment, soft and sweet art thou,
Of the race of Coll and Conn art thou.
My smooth green rush, my laughter sweet,
My little plant in the rocky cleft,
Were it not for the spell on thy tiny feet,
Thou wouldst not here be left,
Not thou.
Of the race of Coll and Conn art thou,
My laughter sweet and low art thou;
As you crow.

Ballad of Douglas Bridge

Francis Carlin (1881–1941)

On Douglas Bridge I met a man,
Who lived adjacent to Strabane,
Before the English hung him high,
For riding with O'Hanlon.

The eyes of him were just as fresh,
As when they burned within the flesh;
And his bootlegs were wide apart,
From riding with O'Hanlon.

'God save you, Sir,' I said with fear,
'You seem a stranger here.'
'Not I,' said he, 'nor any man,
Who rides with Count O'Hanlon.

'I know each glen from north Tyrone,
To Monaghan, and I've been known,
By every clan and parish since,
I rode with Count O'Hanlon.'

'Before that time,' said he to me,
'My fathers owned the land you see;
But they are now among the moors,
A-riding with O'Hanlon.'

'Before that time,' said he with pride,
'My fathers rode where now they ride,
As rapparees, before the time,
Of trouble and O'Hanlon.

'Good night to you, and God be with,
The tellers of the tale and myth,
For they are of the spirit-stuff,
That rides with Count O'Hanlon.

'Good night to you,' said I, 'and
Be with the chargers fairy-shod,
To bear the Ulster heroes forth,
That ride with Count O'Hanlon.'

On Douglas Bridge we parted, but
The gap o' dreams is never shut,
To one whose saddled soul tonight,
Rides out with Count O'Hanlon.

The Stolen Child

William Butler Yeats (1865–1939)

Where dips the rocky highland
Of Sleuth Wood in the lake,
There lies a leafy island
Where flapping herons wake
The drowsy water-rats;
There we've hid our faery vats,
Full of berries
And of reddish stolen cherries.
Come away, O human child!
To the waters and the wild
With a faery, hand in hand,
For the world's more full of weeping than you can understand.

Where the wave of moonlight glosses
The dim grey sands with light,
Far off by furthest Rosses
We foot it all the night,
Weaving olden dances
Mingling hands and mingling glances
Till the moon has taken flight;
To and fro we leap
And chase the frothy bubbles,
While the world is full of troubles
And anxious in its sleep.
Come away, O human child!
To the waters and the wild
With a faery, hand in hand,
For the world's more full of weeping than you can understand.

Where the wandering water gushes
From the hills above Glencar,
In pools among the rushes
That scarce could bathe a star,
We seek for slumbering trout
And whispering in their ears

Give them unquiet dreams;
Leaning softly out
From ferns that drop their tears
Over the young streams.
Come away, O human child!
To the waters and the wild
With a faery, hand in hand,
For the world's more full of weeping than you can understand.

Away with us he's going,
The solemn-eyed:
He'll hear no more the lowing
Of the calves on the warm hillside
Or the kettle on the hob
Sing peace into his breast.
Or see the brown mice bob
Round and round the oatmeal chest.
For he comes, the human child!
To the waters and the wild
With a faery, hand in hand,
From a world more full of weeping than he can understand.

The Song of Wandering Aengus

William Butler Yeats (1865–1939)

I went out to the hazel wood,
Because a fire was in my head,
And cut and peeled a hazel wand
And hooked a berry to a thread;

And when white moths were on the wing,
And moth-like stars were flickering out,
I dropped the berry in a stream
And caught a little silver trout.

When I had laid it on the floor,
I went to blow the fire aflame,
But something rustled on the floor
And someone called me by my name:
It had become a glimmering girl
With apple blossom in her hair
Who called me by my name and ran
And faded through the brightening air.

Though I am old with wandering
Through hollow lands and hill lands,
I will find out where she is gone,
And kiss her lips and take her hands;
And walk among long dappled grass,
And drink till time and times are done
The silver apples of the moon,
The golden apples of the sun.

The Fairy Fiddler

Nora Hopper (1871–1906)

'Tis I go fiddling, fiddling,
    By weedy ways forlorn:
I make the blackbird's music,
    Ere in his breast 'tis born:
The sleeping larks I waken,
    'Twixt the midnight and the morn.

No man alive has seen me,
    But women hear me play,
Sometimes at the door or window,
    Fiddling the soul's away –
The child's soul and the colleen's,
    Out of the covering clay.

None of my fairy kinsmen,
    Make music with me now:
Alone the raths I wander,
    Or ride the whitethorn bough;
But the wild swans they know me,
    And the horse that draws the plough.

The Wayfarer

Pádraic Pearse (1879–1916)

The beauty of the world hath made me sad,
This beauty that will pass;
Sometime my heart hath shaken with great joy,
To see a leaping squirrel in a tree,
Or a red ladybird upon a stalk,
Or little rabbits in a field at evening,
Lit by a slanting sun,
Or some green hill where shadows drifted by,
Some quiet hill where mountainy man hath sown
And soon will reap, near to the gate of Heaven;
Or children with bare feet upon the sands
Or some ebbed sea, or playing on the streets
Of little towns in Connacht,
Things young and happy.
And then my heart hath told me:
These will pass,
Will pass and change, will die and be no more,
Things bright and green,
Things young and happy;
And I have gone upon my way,
Sorrowful.

To My Daughter Betty, the Gift of God

(In the field, before Guillemot, Somme, 4 September 1916)
Thomas Kettle (1880–1916)

In wiser days, my darling rosebud blown
To proud beauty as was your mother's prime,
In that desired, delayed, incredible time,
You'll ask why I abandoned you, my own,
And the dear heart that was your baby throne,
To dice with death. And, oh, they'll give you rhyme
And reason: some will call the thing sublime
And some decry it with a knowing tone.
So here, while the mad guns curse overhead
And tired men sigh, with mud for couch and floor,
Know that we fools, now with the foolish dead,
Died not for flag nor King nor Emperor
But for a dream, born in a herdsman's shed
And for the secret scripture of the poor.

I See His Blood upon the Rose

Joseph Mary Plunkett (1887–1916)

I see his blood upon the rose,
And in the stars the glory of his eyes,
Hid body gleams amid eternal snows,
His tears fall from the skies.
I see his face in every shower;
The thunder and the singing of the birds
Are but his voice – and carven by his power,
Rocks are his written words.
All pathways by his feet are worn,
His strong heart stirs the ever-beating sea,
His crown of thorns is twined with every thorn,
His cross is every tree.

I Shall Not Go to Heaven

Helen Waddell (1889–1965)

I shall not go to Heaven when I die,
But if they'll let me be,
I think I'll take the road I used to know,
That goes by Shere-na-garagh and the sea.
And all day breasting me the wind shall blow,
And I'll hear nothing but the peewits' cry,
And the waves talking in the sea below.

I think it will be winter when I die,
For no one in the north could die in spring;
And all the heather will be dead and grey,
And the bog-cotton will have blown away,
And there will be no yellow on the whin.

But I shall smell the peat,
And when it's almost dark I'll set my feet,
Where a white track goes glimmering to the hills,
And see far up a light…
Would you think Heaven could be so small a thing,
As a lit window on the hills at night?
And come in stumbling from the gloom,
Half-blind, into a firelit room,
Turn and see you,
And there abide.

If it were true,
And if I thought they would let me be,
I almost wish it were tonight I died.

I Know My Love

If I Were a Blackbird

Anon

I am a young maiden and my story is sad,
For once I was courted by a brave sailor lad.
He courted me truly by night and by day,
But now he has left me and gone far away.

Chorus
If I were a blackbird I'd whistle and sing,
And follow the ship that my true love sails in,
And on the top rigging I'd there build my nest,
And pillow my head on his lily-white breast.

He promised to take me to Donnybrook Fair,
To buy me red ribbons to bind up my hair.
And when he'd return from the ocean so wide,
He'd take me and make me his own loving bride.

His parents, they slight me and will not agree,
That I and my sailor boy married should be.
But when he comes home I will greet him with joy,
And I'll take to my bosom my dear sailor boy.

I Know My Love

Anon

I know my love by his way of walking,
And I know my love by his way of talking,
And I know my love dressed in his jersey blue,
And if my love leaves me what will I do?

Chorus
And still she cried, 'I love him the best,
And a tiring mind can know no rest.'
And still she cried, 'Bonny boys are few,
And if my love leaves me what will I do?'

There is a dance house down in Mardyke,
And there my true love goes every night,
And takes a strange one upon his knee,
And don't you think now that vexes me?

Johnny, I Hardly Knew Ye

Anon

'Sulloon' in the sixth stanza is Ceylon, present-day Sri Lanka.

While going the road to sweet Athy,
    Hurroo! Hurroo!
While going the road to sweet Athy,
    Hurroo! Hurroo!
While going the road to sweet Athy,
A stick in my hand and a drop in my eye,
A doleful damsel I heard cry,
    'Och, Johnny, I hardly knew ye!'

Chorus
'With your drums and guns and guns and drums, Hurroo! Hurroo!
With your drums and guns and guns and drums, Hurroo! Hurroo!
With your drums and guns and guns and drums,
The enemy nearly slew ye,
My darling dear, you look so queer;
    Och, Johnny, I hardly knew ye!'

'Where are your eyes that looked so mild?
    Hurroo! Hurroo!
Where are your eyes that looked so mild?
    Hurroo! Hurroo!
Where are your eyes that looked so mild
When my poor heart you first beguiled?
Why did you run from me and the child?
    Och, Johnny, I hardly knew ye!

'Where are the legs with which you run?
    Hurroo! Hurroo!
Where are the legs with which you run?
    Hurroo! Hurroo!'
Where are the legs with which you run?
When first you went to carry a gun –
Indeed your dancing days are done!
    Och, Johnny, I hardly knew ye!

'It grieved my heart to see you sail,
 Hurroo! Hurroo!
It grieved my heart to see you sail,
 Hurroo! Hurroo!
It grieved my heart to see you sail,
Though from my heart you took leg-bail,
Like a cod you're doubled up head and tail,
 Och, Johnny, I hardly knew ye!'

'You haven't an arm and you haven't a leg,
 Hurroo! Hurroo!
You haven't an arm and you haven't a leg,
 Hurroo! Hurroo!
You haven't an arm and you haven't a leg,
You're an eyeless, noseless, chickenless egg;
You'll have to be put out with a bowl to beg,
 Och, Johnny, I hardly knew ye!

'I'm happy for to see you home,
 Hurroo! Hurroo!
I'm happy for to see you home,
 Hurroo! Hurroo!
I'm happy for to see you home,
All from the island of Sulloon,
So low in flesh, so high in bone,
 Och, Johnny, I hardly knew ye!

'But sad as it is to see you so,
 Hurroo! Hurroo!
But sad as it is to see you so,
 Hurroo! Hurroo!
But sad as it is to see you so,
And to think of you now as an object of woe,
Your Peggy'll keep ye on as her beau,
 Och, Johnny, I hardly knew ye!'

The Rose of Mooncoin

Seamus Kavanagh (d. 1964)

How sweet 'tis to roam by the sunny Suir stream,
And hear the dove coo 'neath the morning sunbeam,
Where the thrush and the robin their sweet notes entwine,
On the banks of the Suir that flows down by Moincoin.

Chorus
Flow on lovely river, flow gently along,
By your waters so clear sounds the lark's merry song,
On your green banks I'll wander where first I did join,
With you, lovely Molly, the Rose of Mooncoin

Oh! Molly, dear Molly, it breaks my fond heart,
To know that we two for ever must part.
I'll think of you, Molly, while sun and moon shine,
On the banks of the Suir that flows down by Mooncoin.

She sailed far away o'er the dark rolling foam,
Far away from the hills of her dear Irish home,
Where the fisherman sports with his small boat and line,
By the banks of the Suir that flows down by Moincoin.

Come, Come, Beautiful Eileen

Anon

Now Eileen O'Grady's a real Irish lady,
I'm longing to call her my own.
I'll not be contented, until she has consented,
To be Mistress Barney Malone.
I met this fair treasure, while walking for pleasure,
She looked up at me, then she cried,
Without any warning, 'The top of the morning!'
And then up to her I replied:

Chorus
Come, come, beautiful Eileen,
Come for a drive with me,
Over the mountain, down by the fountain,
Over the high road and down by the low road.
Make up your mind, don't be unkind,
And we'll drive to Castlebar.
To the road I'm no stranger,
For you there's no danger,
So hop like a bird on my old jaunting car.

But Eileen said, 'No sir. With you I won't go, sir.
Don't think it ungrateful of me.
I'd rather be walking, than have people talking,
You know what the story would be.'
'Now, Eileen my jewel, don't treat me so cruel
To treat me this way is a shame.
Give over your blarney
And say I'm your Barney
And don't keep me waiting in vain.'

The Dawning of the Day

Anon

One morning early I walked forth by the margin of Lough Leane;
The sunshine dressed the trees in green and summer bloom'd again.
I left the town and wandered on, through fields all green and gay,
And who should I meet but a colleen sweet, at the dawning of the day.

No cap nor coat this maiden wore; her neck and feet were bare.
Down to the grass in ringlets fell her glossy golden hair.
A milking pail was in her hand; she was lovely, young and gay.
She bore the palm from Venus bright by the dawning of the day.

On a mossy bank I sat me down with the maiden by my side.
With gentle words I courted her and asked her to be my bride.
She said, 'Young man, don't bring me blame,' and swiftly turned away,
And the morning light was shining bright at the dawning of the day.

Pearl of the White Breast

(from the Irish)
Sir George Petrie (1789–1866)

There's a colleen fair as May,
For a year and for a day,
I've sought by every way her heart to gain.
There's no art of tongue or eye,
Fond youths with maidens try,
But I've tried with ceaseless sigh, yet tried in vain.
If to France or far-off Spain,
She'd cross the watery main,
To see her face again the sea I'd brave.
And if 'tis heaven's decree,
That mine she may not be,
May the Son of Mary me in mercy save!

O thou blooming milk-white dove,
To whom I've given true love,
Do not ever thus reprove my constancy.
There are maidens would be mine,
With wealth in hand and kine,
If my heart would but incline to turn from thee.
But a kiss with welcome bland,
And a touch of they dear hand,
Are all that I'd demand, wouldst though not spurn.
For if not mine, dear girl!
O Snowy-Breasted Pearl!
May I never from the fair, with life, return!

Molly Bawn

Samuel Lover (1797–1868)

O Molly Bawn, why leave me pining,
All lonely waiting here for you,
While the stars above are brightly shining,
Because they've nothing else to do.
Now the pretty flowers were made to bloom, dear,
And the pretty stars were made to shine,
And the pretty girls were made for boys' arms
And maybe you were meant for mine.

The wicked watchdog here is snarling.
He takes me for a thief, you see,
For he knows I'd steal you, Molly darling,
And then transported I should be.
O Molly Bawn, why leave me pining,
All lonely waiting here for you,
While the stars above are brightly shining,
Because they've nothing else to do.

The Lark in the Clear Air

Samuel Ferguson (1810–86)

Dear thoughts are in my mind and my soul soars enchanted,
As I hear the sweet lark sing in the clear air of the day.
For a tender beaming smile to my hope has been granted,
And tomorrow she shall hear all my fond heart would say.

I shall tell her all my love, all my soul's adoration,
And I think she will hear me and she will not say me nay.
It is this that gives my soul all its joyous elation,
As I hear the sweet lark sing in the clear air of the day.

Dear Dark Head (from the Irish)

Samuel Ferguson (1810–86)

Put your head, darling, darling, darling,
Your darling black head my heart above;
O mouth of honey, with the thyme for fragrance,
Who, with heart in breast, could deny you love?

Oh, many and many a young girl for me is pining.
Letting her locks of gold to the cold wind free,
For me, the foremost of our gay young fellows;
But I'd leave a hundred, pure love, for thee!

Then put your head, darling, darling, darling,
Your darling black head my heart above;
O mouth of honey, with the thyme for fragrance,
Who, with heart in breast, could deny you love?

The Spinning Wheel

John Francis Waller (1810–94)

Mellow the moonlight to shine is beginning.
Close by the window young Eileen is spinning.
Bent over the fire her blind grandmother, sitting,
Is crooning and moaning and drowsily knitting.

'Eileen, a chara, I hear someone tapping.'
'Tis the ivy, dear mother, against the glass flapping.'
'Eily, I surely hear somebody sighing.'
'Tis the sound, mother dear, of the summer wind dying.'

Merrily, cheerily, noiselessly whirring,
Swings the wheels, spins the wheel, while the foot's stirring.
Sprightly and brightly and airily ringing,
Thrills the sweet voice of the young maiden singing.

'What's that noise that I hear at the window, I wonder?'
''Tis the little birds chirping the holly-bush under.'
'What makes you be shoving and moving your stool on,
And singing, all wrong, that old song of "The Coolun"?'

There's a form at the casement – the form of her true love –
And he whispers, with face bent, 'I'm waiting for you, love.
Get up on the stool, through the lattice step lightly,
We'll rove in the grove while the moon's shining brightly.'

Merrily, cheerily, noiselessly whirring,
Swings the wheels, spins the wheel, while the foot's stirring.
Sprightly and brightly and airily ringing,
Thrills the sweet voice of the young maiden singing.

The maid shakes her head, on her lips lays her fingers,
Steals up from her seat – longs to go and yet lingers.
A frightened glance turns to her drowsy grandmother,
Puts one foot on the stool, spins the wheel with the other.

Lazily, easily, swings now the wheel round;
Slowly and lowly is heard now the reel's sound;
Noiseless and light to the lattice above her,
The maid steps – then leaps to the arms of her lover.

Slower and slower and slower the wheel swings;
Lower and lower and lower the reel rings.
Ere the reel and the wheel stopped their ringing and moving,
Through the grove the young lovers by moonlight are strolling.

The Irish Peasant Girl

Charles Joseph Kickham (1828–1882)

She lived beside the Anner,
At the foot of Sliev-na-man,
A gentle peasant girl,
With mild eyes like the dawn.
Her lips were dewy rosebuds;
Her teeth of pearls rare,
And a snow-drift 'neath a beechen bough,
Her neck and nut-brown hair.

How pleasant 'twas to meet her,
On Sunday, when the bell,
Was filling with its mellow tones,
Lone wood and grassy dell.
And when at eve young maidens,
Strayed the river bank along,
The widow's brown-haired daughter,
Was loveliest of the throng.

O brave, brave Irish girls –
We may well call you brave –
Sure the least of all your perils,
Is the stormy ocean wave,
When you leave our quiet valleys
And cross the Atlantic's foam
To hoard your hard-won earnings
For the helpless ones at home.

'Write word to my own mother –
Say we'll meet with God above,
And tell my little brothers,
I send them all my love.
May the angels ever guard them,
Is their dying sister's prayer' –
And folded in the letter,
Was a braid of nut-brown hair.

Ah, cold and well-nigh callous,
This weary heart has grown,
For thy helpless fate, dear Ireland,
And for sorrows of my own.
Yet a tear my eye will moisten,
When by Anner side I stray,
For the lily of the mountain foot,
That withered far away.

The Garden where the Praties Grow

Johnny Patterson (1840–89)

Have you ever been in love, me boys, or have you felt the pain?
I'd sooner be in jail myself than be in love again,
For the girl I loved was beautiful, I'd have you all to know
And I met her in the garden where the praties grow.

Chorus
She was just the sort of creature, boys, that nature did intend
To walk right through the world, me boys, without the Grecian bend.
Nor did she wear a chignon, I'd have you all to know,
And I met her in the garden where the praties grow.

Says I, 'My pretty Kathleen, I'm tired of single life
And if you've no objection, sure I'll make you my sweet wife.'
She answered me right modestly and curtsied very low,
'Oh, you're welcome to the garden where the praties grow.'

Says I, 'My pretty Kathleen, I hope that you'll agree.'
She wasn't like your city girls who'd say, 'You're making free.'
Says she, 'I'll ax my parents and tomorrow I'll let you know,
If you'll meet me in the garden where the praties grow.

Well, the parents they consented and we're blessed with children three,
Two boys just like their mother and a girl the image of me
And now we're going to train them up in the way they ought to go,
For to dig out in the garden where the praties grow.

Maire, My Girl

John Keegan Casey (1846–70)

Over the dim blue hills,
Strays a wild river.
Over the dim blue hills,
Rests my heart ever.
Dearer and brighter,
Than jewels and pearl,
Dwells she in beauty there,
Maire my girl.

Down upon Claris heath,
Shines the soft berry.
On the brown harvest tree,
Drops the red cherry.
Sweeter thy honey lips,
Softer the curl,
Straying adown thy cheeks,
Maire my girl.

'Twas on an April eve,
That I first met her.
Many an eve shall pass,
Ere I forget her.
Since my young heart has been,
Wrapped in a whirl,
Thinking and dreaming of,
Maire my girl.

She is too kind and fond,
Ever to grieve me.
She has too pure a heart,
E'er to deceive me.
Were I Tyrconnel's chief,
Or Desmond's earl,
Life would be dark, wanting,
Maire my girl.

Over the dim blue hills,
Strays a wild river.
Over the dim blue hills,
Rests my heart ever.
Dearer and brighter,
Than jewels and pearl,
Dwells she in beauty there,
Maire my girl.

Little Brigid Flynn

Percy French (1854–1920)

I've a nice slated house and a cow or two at grass.
I've a plant garden running by the door.
I've a shelter for the hens and a stable for the ass,
And what does a man want more.
I dunno, maybe so,
And a bachelor is aisy and he's free.
But I've lots to look after,
And I'm living all alone
And there's no one looking after me.

Me father often tells me I should go and have a try,
To get a girl that owns a bit of land;
I know the way he says it that there's someone in his eye,
And me mother has the whole thing planned.
I dunno, maybe so,
And 'twould mollify them greatly to agree;
But there's little Brigid Flynn,
Sure it's her I want to win,
Though she never throws an eye at me.

Oh! there's a little girl who is worth her weight in gold,
An' that's a dacent dowry don't you see;
And I mean to go and ax her as soon as I get bold,
If she'll come and have an eye on me.
I dunno – will she go?
But I'd like to have her sittin' on my knee,
And I'd sing like a thrush
On a hawthorn bush
If she'd come and have an eye for me.

John-John

Thomas MacDonagh (1878–1916)

I dreamt last night of you, John-John,
And thought you called to me;
And when I woke this morning, John,
Yourself I hoped to see;
But I was all alone, John-John,
Though still I heard your call:
I put my boots and bonnet on,
And took my Sunday shawl,
And went, full sure to find you, John,
To Nenagh fair.

The fair was just the same as then,
Five years ago today,
When first you left the thimble men,
And came with me away;
For there again were thimble men,
And shooting galleries,
And card-trick men and Maggie men,
Of all sorts and degrees –
But not a sight of you, John-John,
Was anywhere.

I turned my face to home again,
And called myself a fool,
To think you'd leave the thimble men,
And live again by rule,
And go to Mass and keep the fast,
And till the little patch:
My wish to have you home was past,
Before I raised the latch,
And pushed the door and saw you, John,
Sitting down there.

How cool you came in there, begad,
As if you owned the place!

But rest yourself there now, my lad,
'Tis good to see your face;
My dream is out, and now by it,
I think I know my mind:
At six o'clock this house you'll quit,
And leave no grief behind –
But until six o'clock, John-John,
My bit you'll share.

The neighbour's shame of me began,
When first I brought you in,
To wed and keep a tinker man,
They thought a kind of sin;
But now this three year since you've gone,
'Tis pity me they do,
And that I'd rather have, John-John,
Than that they'd pity you.
Pity for me and you, John-John,
I could not bear.

Oh, you're my husband right enough,
But what's the good of that?
You know you never were the stuff,
To be the cottage cat,
To watch the fire and hear me lock,
The door and put out Shep –
But there now, it is six o'clock,
And time for you to step.
God bless and keep you far, John-John!
And that's my prayer.

He Wishes
for the Cloths of Heaven

William Butler Yeats (1865–1939)

Had I the heavens' embroidered cloths
Enwrought with golden and silver light,
The blue and the dim and the dark cloths
Of night and light and the half-light
I would spread the cloths under your feet:
But I, being poor, have only my dreams;
I have spread my dreams under your feet;
Tread softly because you tread on my dreams.

The Salley Gardens

William Butler Yeats (1865–1939)

Down by the salley gardens my love and I did meet.
She passed the salley gardens with little snow-white feet.
She bid me take love easy, as the leaves grow on the tree
But I, being young and foolish, with her would not agree.

In a field by the river my love and I did stand
And on my leaning shoulder she laid her snow-white hand.
She bid me take life easy, as the grass grows on the weirs
But I was young and foolish, and now am full of tears.

Macushla

Josephine V. Rowe (fl. 1910)

Macushla! Macushla! your sweet voice is calling,
Calling me softly again and again.
Macushla! Macushla! I hear its dear pleading,
My blue-eyed Macushla, I hear it in vain.

Macushla! Macushla! your white arms are reaching,
I feel them enfolding, caressing me still.
Fling them out from the darkness, my lost love Macushla,
Let them find me and bind me again if they will.

Macushla! Macushla! your red lips are saying,
That death is a dream and love is for aye,
Then awaken, Macushla, awake from your dreaming,
My blue-eyed Macushla, awaken to stay.

All the Sweet Buttermilk

The Next Market Day

Anon

A maid goin' to Comber, her markets to larn,
To sell for her mammy three hanks o' fine yarn,
She met with a young man along the highway,
Which caused this young damsel to dally and stray.
'Sit ye beside me, I mean ye no harm.
Sit ye beside me this new tune to larn.
Here is three guineas your Mammy to pay,
So lay by your yarn till the next market day.'

They sat down together, the grass it was green,
The day was the fairest that ever was seen.
'Oh the look in your eye beats a mornin' o' May,
I could sit by your side till the next market day.'
This young maid went home and the words that he said,
And the air that he played her still rang in her head.
She says, 'I'll go find him by land or by sea,
Till he larns me that tune called "The Next Market Day".'

The Bard of Armagh

Anon

Oh! list to the lay of a poor Irish harper,
And scorn not the strains of his poor withered hand,
But remember his fingers could once move more sharper,
To raise up the memory of his poor native land.
It was long before the shamrock, our green isle's loved emblem,
Was crushed in its beauty 'neath the Saxon lion's paw.
I was called by the colleens of the village and valley:
Bold Phelim Brady, the Bard of Armagh.

How I long for to muse on the days of my boyhood,
Though four score and three years have flitted since then.
Still it gives sweet reflections, as every young joy should,
Thou merry-hearted boys make the best of old men.
At pattern or fair I could twist my shillelagh,
Or trip through the jig with my brogues bound with straw,
Whilst all the pretty maidens around me assembled,
Loved Bold Phelim Brady, the Bard of Armagh.

Although I have travelled this wide world over,
Yet Erin's my home and a parent to me.
Then oh! let the ground that my old bones shall cover,
Be cut from the soil that is trod by the free.
And when Sergeant Death in his cold arms shall embrace me,
O lull me to sleep with sweet Erin go bragh.
By the side of my Kathleen, my young wife, O place me.
Then forget Phelim Brady, the Bard of Armagh.

The Darling Girl from Clare

Anon

We were sittin' on the wall upon a Sunday,
To watch the girls go by,
And thinkin' we'd be marrit to one one day,
When Kate Flynn caught our eye.
Oh, man! she was the makin's of a fairy,
And it made each boyo swear,
'There's not one girl in the wide, wide world
Like the girl from the County Clare!'

Chorus
And ev'ry man had got the finest plan
You ever see now – barrin' me now,
Ev'ry day there's one of them would say
That she'll agree now – you'll see now;
All night they'd fight,
As to which o' them was right,
In the colour of her eyes and hair,
But not a word from me was ever heard,
About the darlin' girl from Clare!

Says Casey: "'Tis the father I'll be plazin',
I'll tell him of the land I've tilled,
I'll tell him of the cattle I have grazin'
And the house I mean to build;
And whin he sees the arable and pasture,
And the fat stock feedin' there,
An' the hens an' the chickens,
Ye may go to the dickens,
For the girl from the County Clare.'

Chorus
So ev'ry man had got the finest plan
Ye ever see now– barrin' me now,
Ev'ry day there's one of them would say
That she'll agree now –you'll see now.

Says I to meself,
Though I haven't got the pelf,
Of brass I've got my share,
And so I know the way they ought to go,
About the darlin' girl from Clare.

Says Sweeney, 'She'll be coming to the shop here
To buy some sort of thing,
I'll ax her if she has a mind to stop there,
And should I buy the ring:
An' whin she sees the curtains on the windas,
An' the clock on the stair
Keepin' time to the minit,
No one else will be in it
With the darlin' girl from Clare!'

Chorus
So ev'ry man had got the finest plan
Ye ever see now – barrin' me now,
Ev'ry day there's one of them would say,
That she'll agree now – you'll see now;
Thinks I, 'Ye may stop
Till yer dead in yer shop,
An' not a hair she'll care, Wid all yer gold
Ye'll never hold a hold,
Upon the darlin' girl from Clare.'

I never said a single word about her,
But I met the girl that day,
I told her I could never live widout her,
An' what had she to say?
She said that I might go and see her father:
I met him then and there,
An' in less than an hour
We war fightin' for the dower
Of the darlin' girl from Clare!

Chorus
So ev'ry man had got the finest plan
Ye ever see now – barrin' me now,
Ev'ry day there's one of them would say
That she'll agree now – you'll see now;
But late last night
When the moon was bright
I axed her if she'd share
Me joy an' me sorra' –
An' begorra! on tomorro'
I'll be married to the girl from Clare!

The Spanish Lady

Anon

As I walked down through Dublin city,
At the hour of twelve in the night,
Who should I spy but a Spanish lady,
Washing her feet by candlelight?
First she dipped them, then she dried them,
Over a fire of ambery coal.
Never in all my life did I see,
A maid so neat about the sole.

I stopped to peep but the watchman passed,
And says: 'Young fellow, the night is late.
Get home to bed or I'll wrastle you,
At double trot through the Bridewell gate!'
So I waved a kiss to the Spanish lady,
Hot as the fire of cramesy coal.
I've seen dark maids though never one,
So white and neat about the sole.

O, she's too rich for a Poddle swaddy,
With her tortoise comb and mantle fine.
A Hellfire buck would fit her better,
Drinking brandy and claret wine.
I'm just a decent College sizar,
Poor as a sod of smouldery coal;
How would I dress the Spanish lady
And she no neat about the sole?

O, she'd make a mott for the provost marshal,
Or a wife for the mayor on his coach so high,
Or a queen for Andalusia,
Kicking her heel in the cardinal's eye.
I'm blue as cockles, brown as herrings,
Over a grid of glimmery coal,
And all because of the Spanish lady,
So mortal neat about the sole.

232

I wandered north and I wandered south,
By Golden Lane and Patrick's Close,
The Coombe, Smithfield and Stoneybatter,
Back to Napper Tandy's house.
Old age has laid its hand upon me,
Cold as a fire of ashy coal,
And where is the lovely Spanish lady,
That maid so neat about the sole.

Cockles and Mussels

Anon

In Dublin's fair city,
Where the girls are so pretty,
I first set my eyes on sweet Mollie Malone.
She wheeled her wheelbarrow,
Through streets broad and narrow,
Crying, 'Cockles and mussels, alive, alive, oh!'

Chorus
Alive, alive, oh!
Alive, alive, oh!
Crying, 'Cockles and mussels, alive, alive, oh!'

She was a fishmonger,
But sure 'twas no wonder,
For so were her mother and father before.
And they both wheeled their barrow,
Through streets broad and narrow,
Crying, 'Cockles and mussels, alive, alive, oh!'

She died of a fever,
And none could relieve her,
And that was the end of sweet Mollie Malone,
But her ghost wheels her barrow,
Through streets broad and narrow,
Crying, 'Cockles and mussels, alive, alive, oh!'

At Oranmore

Anon

At Oranmore in the County Galway,
One pleasant evening the month of May,
I spied a damsel, she was young and handsome –
Her beauty fair took my breath away.

Chorus
She wore no jewels nor costly diamonds,
No paint and powder, no, none at all.
But she wore a bonnet with ribbon on it,
And round her shoulders was a Galway shawl.

We kept on walking; she kept on talking,
Till her father's cottage came into view.
Says she: 'Come in, sir, and meet my father
And play to please him, "The Foggy Dew".'

She sat me down beside the hearthstone;
I could see her father, he was six feet tall.
And soon her mother had the kettle singing –
All I could think off was the Galway shawl.

I played 'The Blackbird' and 'The Stack of Barley'
'Rodney's Glory' and 'The Foggy Dew'.
She sang each note like an Irish linnet,
Whilst the tears stood in her eyes of blue.

'Twas early, early all in the morning,
When I hit the road for old Donegal.
She said: 'Goodbye, sir.' She cried and kissed me,
And my heart remained with that Galway shawl.

My Own Lovely Lee

Anon

How oft in do my thoughts in their fancy take flight,
To the home of my childhood away,
To the days when each patriot vision seemed bright,
'Ere I dream'd that those joys should decay.
When my heart was as light as the wild winds that blow,
Down the Mardyke through each elm tree,
Where I sported and played 'neath each green leafy shade,
On the banks of my own lovely Lee.
Where I sported and played 'neath each green leafy shade
On the banks of my own lovely Lee.

And then in the springtime of laughter and song,
Can I ever forget the sweet hours,
With the friends of my youth as we rambled along,
'Mongst the green mossy banks and wild flowers.
Then too when the evening sun sinking to rest,
Shed its golden light over the sea,
The maid with her lover the wild daisies press'd
On the banks of my own lovely Lee.
The maid with her lover the wild daisies press'd
On the banks of my own lovely Lee.

'Tis a beautiful land this dear isle of song;
Its gems shed their light on the world,
And her faithful sons bore through ages of wrong,
The standard St Patrick unfurled.
Oh! would I were there with the friends I love best,
And my fond bosom's partner with me.
We'd roam thy banks o'er and when weary we'd rest,
By thy waters, my own lovely Lee.
We'd roam thy banks o'er and when weary we'd rest,
By thy waters, my own lovely Lee.

Oh! what joys should be mine ere this life should decline,
To seek shells on the sea-girdled shore,
While the steel-feathered eagle, oft splashing the brine,
Brings longing for freedom once more.
Oh! all that on earth I wish for or crave,
Is that my last crimson drop be for thee,
To moisten the grass of my forefathers' grave,
On the banks of my own lovely Lee.
To moisten the grass of my forefathers' grave,
On the banks of my own lovely Lee.

The Curragh of Kildare

Anon

The winter it is past, and the summer's come at last,
The small birds are singing in the trees;
Their little hearts are glad, oh but mine is very sad,
For my true love is far away from me.

The rose and the briar and the water running by,
Are heaven for the linnet and the bee.
Their little hearts are blessed, oh but mine is not at rest,
For my true love is far away from me.

A livery I will wear and I'll comb back my hair,
And in a velvet green I will appear.
And it's straight I will go there to the Curragh of Kildare,
For it's there I'll find tidings of my dear.

I'll wear a cap of black with a frill around my neck,
Gold rings on each finger I will wear.
It's this I undertake for my own true love's sake;
She resides at the Curragh of Kildare.

My love is like the sun that in the firmament doth run,
And always proves so constant and so true;
But hers is like the moon that wanders up and down,
And each month becomes something quite new.

The Low-Backed Car

Samuel Lover (1797–1868)

When first I saw sweet Peggy,
'Twas on a market day;
A low-backed car she drove and sat,
Upon a truss of hay.
But when that hay was blooming grass,
And decked with flowers of spring,
No flow'r was there that could compare,
With the blooming girl I sing.
As she sat in the low-backed car –
The man at the turnpike bar
Never asked for the toll
But just rubbed his ould poll
And looked after the low-backed car.

In battle's wild commotion,
The proud and mighty Mars,
With hostile scythes demands his tithes,
Of death – in warlike cars.
While Peggy, peaceful goddess,
Has darts in her bright eye,
That knock men down in the market town,
As right and left they fly –
While she sits in her low-backed car –
Than battle more dangerous far;
For the doctor's art
Cannot cure the heart
That is hit from that low-backed car.

Sweet Peggy, round her car, sir,
Has strings of ducks and geese,
But the scores of hearts she slaughters,
By far outnumbers these.
While she among her poultry sits,
Just like a turtle-dove,
Well worth the cage, I do engage,
Of the blooming god of love!
While she sits in her low-backed car –
The lovers come near and far,
And envy the chicken,
That Peggy is pickin'
As she sits in the low-backed car.

Oh, I'd rather own that car, sir,
With Peggy by my side,
Than a coach-and-four and gold galore,
And a lady for my bride.
For the lady would sit forninst me,
On a cushion made with taste,
While Peggy would sit beside me,
With my arm around her waist.
While we drove in the low-backed car –
To be married by Father Maher,
Oh, my heart would beat high,
At her glance and her sigh –
Though it beat in a low-backed car.

Kitty of Coleraine

Charles Dawson Shanly (1811–75)

As beautiful Kitty one morning was tripping,
With a pitcher of milk for the fair of Coleraine,
When she saw me she stumbled, the pitcher down tumbled,
And all the sweet buttermilk watered the plain.
'Oh, what shall I do now? 'Twas looking at you now!
I'm sure such a pitcher I'll ne'er see again.
'Twas the pride of my dairy. O, Barney McLeary,
You're sent as a plague to the girls of Coleraine.'

I sat down beside her and gently did chide her
That such a misfortune should cause her such pain;
A kiss then I gave her and before I did leave her,
She vowed for such pleasure she'd break it again.
'Twas the haymaking season – I can't tell the reason –
Misfortunes will never come single 'tis plain!
For very soon after poor Kitty's disaster
The devil a pitcher was whole in Coleraine.

The Rose of Tralee

William Mulchinock (1820–64)

The pale moon was rising above the green mountain;
The sun was declining beneath the blue sea,
When I stray'd with my love to the pure crystal fountain,
That stands in the beautiful vale of Tralee.

She was lovely and fair as the rose of the summer,
Yet 'twas not her beauty alone that won me.
Oh, no, 'twas the truth in her eyes ever dawning,
That made me love Mary, the Rose of Tralee.

The cool shades of evening their mantle were spreading,
And Mary, all smiling, sat listening to me,
The moon through the valley her pale rays was shedding,
When I won the heart of the Rose of Tralee.

Tho' lovely and fair as the rose of the summer,
Yet 'twas not her beauty alone that won me.
Oh, no, 'twas the truth in her eyes ever dawning,
That made me love Mary, the Rose of Tralee.

Slievenamon

Charles J. Kickham (1828–82)

All alone, all alone, by the wave-washed shore,
All alone in the crowded hall.
The hall it is gay and the waves they are grand
But my heart is not there at all.
It flies far away, by night and by day,
To the times and the joys that are gone,
But I never shall forget the sweet maiden I met,
In the valley near Slievenamon.

It was not the grace of her queenly air,
Nor her cheek of the rose's glow,
Nor her soft black eyes nor her flowing hair,
Nor was it her lily-white brow.
'Twas the soul of truth and of melting ruth,
And the smile like the summer dawn,
That stole my heart away, one mild summer day,
In the valley near Slievenamon.

In the festive hall by the star-watched shore,
My restless spirit cries:
'My love, oh my love, shall I ne'er see you more,
And, my land, will you ever uprise?'
By night and by day I ever, ever pray,
While lonely my life flows on,
To see our flag unrolled and my true love to unfold,
In the valley near Slievenamon.

The Stone outside Dan Murphy's Door

Johnny Patterson (1840–89)

There's a sweet garden spot in our memory,
It's the place we were born in and reared,
It's long years ago since left it,
But return there we will if we're spared,
Our friends and companions of childhood,
Would assemble each night near a score,
Round Dan Murphy's shop and how often we sat,
On the stone outside Dan Murphy's door.

Chorus
Those days in our hearts we will cherish,
Contented although we were poor,
And the songs that were sung,
In the days we were young,
On the stone outside Dan Murphy's door.

When our day's work was over we'd meet there,
In the winter or spring just the same,
Then the boys and the girls all together,
Would join in some innocent game.
Dan Murphy would take down his fiddle,
While his daughter looked after the store,
The music did ring and sweet songs we would sing,
On the stone outside Dan Murphy's door.

Back again will our thoughts often wander,
To the scenes of our childhood's home,
The friends and companions we left there,
It was poverty caused us to roam.
Since then in this life we have prospered,
But still in our hearts we feel sore.
For memory will fly to those days long gone by,
And the stone outside Dan Murphy's door.

Eileen Oge

Percy French (1854–1920)

Eilleen Oge, and that the darlin's name is;
Through the barony her features, they were famous.
If we loved her who is there to blame us,
For wasn't she the Pride of Petravore?
But her beauty made us all so shy;
Not a man could look her in the eye.
Boys, oh, boys! Sure that's the reason why,
We're in mournin' for the Pride of Petravore.

Chorus
Eileen Oge, me heart is growin' grey,
Ever since the day you wander'd far away.
Eileen Oge, there's good fish in the say,
But there's no one like the Pride of Petravore.

Friday at the fair of Ballintubber,
Eileen met McGrath, the cattle jobber,
I'd like to set me mark upon the robber,
For he stole away the Pride of Petravore.
He never seem'd to see the girl at all,
Even when she ogl'd him underneath her shawl,
Lookin' big and masterful when he was lookin' small,
Most provokin' for the Pride of Petravore.

So it went as it was in the beginning;
Eileen Oge was bent upon the winning.
Big McGrath contentedly was grinning,
Being courted by the Pride of Petravore.
Sez he, 'I know a girl could knock you into fits.'
At that Eileen nearly lost her wits.
The upshot of the ruction was that now the robber sits
With his arm around the Pride of Petravore.

Boys oh, boys! With fate 'tis hard to grapple.
Of my eye 'tis Eileen was the apple,
And now to see her walkin' to the chapel,
Wid the hardest-featured man in Petravore.
And, now, me boys, this is all I have to say,
When you do your courtin' make no display.
For they're mostly like the Pride of Petravore,
If you want them to run after you just walk the other way.

Come Back, Paddy Reilly

Percy French (1854–1920)

The Garden of Eden has vanished they say,
But I know the lie of it still;
Just turn to the left at the bridge of Finea,
And stop when halfway to Cootehill.
'Tis there you will find it; I know sure enough,
When fortune has come to my call.
Oh! the grass it is green around Ballyjamesduff,
And the blue sky is over it all;
And tones that are tender and tones that are gruff,
Are whispering over the sea:
'Come back, Paddy Reilly, to Ballyjamesduff;
Come home, Paddy Reilly, to me.'

My mother once told me that when I was born,
The day that I first saw the light,
I looked down the street on that very first morn,
And gave a great crow of delight.
Now most new-born babies appear in a huff,
And start with a sorrowful squall,
But I knew I was born in Ballyjamesduff,
And that's why I smiled on them all.
The baby's a man now, he's toilworn and tough,
Still, whispers come over the sea:
'Come back, Paddy Reilly, to Ballyjamesduff;
Come home, Paddy Reilly, to me.'

The night that we danced by the light of the moon,
Wid Phil to the fore wid his flute.
When Phil threw his lip over 'Come Again Soon',
He'd dance the foot out o' your boot!
The day that I took Long Magee by the scruff,
For slanderin' Rosie Kilrain,
Then marchin' him straight out of Ballyjamesduff,
Assisted him into a drain,

Oh sweet are my dreams, as the dudeen I puff,
Of whispering over the sea:
'Come back, Paddy Reilly, to Ballyjamesduff;
Come home, Paddy Reilly, to me.'

I've struck oil at last! I've struck work and, I vow,
I've struck some remarkable clothes.
I've struck a policeman for saying that now,
I'd go back on my beautiful Rose.
The belles they may blarney, the boys they are bluff;
But this I will always maintain,
No place in the world is like Ballyjamesduff,
No girl like Rosie Kilrain.
I've paid for my passage, the sea may be rough,
But borne on each breeze there will be:
'Come back, Paddy Reilly, to Ballyjamesduff;
Come home, Paddy Reilly, to me.'

The Mountains of Mourne

Percy French (1854–1920)

Oh, Mary, this London's a wonderful sight,
Wid the people here workin' by day and by night.
They don't sow potatoes nor barley nor wheat,
But there's gangs of them diggin' for gold in the street.
At least, when I axed them, that's what I was told,
So I just took a hand at this diggin' for gold.
But for all that I found there, I might as well be,
Where the Mountains of Mourne sweep down to the sea.

I believe that, when writin', a wish you expressed,
As to how the fine ladies in London were dressed.
Well, if you'll believe me, when axed to a ball,
They don't wear a top to their dresses at all!
Oh, I've seen them meself, and you could not, in truth,
Say if they were bound for a ball or a bath…
Don't be startin' them fashions, Mary Machree,
Where the Mountains of Mourne sweep down to the sea.

You remember young Peter O'Loughlin, of course –
Well he's over here now at the head o' the force.
I met him today, I was crossin' the Strand,
And he stopped the whole street wid one wave of his hand.
And there we stood talking of days that are gone,
While the whole population of London looked on;
But for all his great powers he's wishful like me,
To be back where the dark Mourne sweeps down to the sea.

There's beautiful girls here – oh, never mind –
With beautiful shapes nature never designed.
And lovely complexions, all roses and crame
But O'Loughlin remarked with regard to the same:
'That if at those roses you happened to sip
The colour might all come away on your lip.'
So I'll wait for the wild rose that's waiting for me
Where the Mountains of Mourne sweep down to the sea.

The Queen of Connemara

Francis Fahy (1854-1935)

Oh my boat can swiftly float,
In the teeth of wind and weather,
And outsail the fastest hooker,
Between Galway and Kinsale.
When the white rim of the ocean,
And the wild waves rush together,
Oh she rides in her pride,
Like a sea bird in a gale.

Chorus
She's neat, oh, she's sweet,
She's a beauty in every line,
The queen of Connemara,
Is this bounding barque of mine.

When she's loaded down with fish,
Till the water lips the gunwale,
Not a drop she'll take aboard her,
That would wash a fly away.
From the fleet she speeds out quickly,
Like a greyhound from her kennel,
Till she lands her silvery store,
The first on old Kinvara Quay.

There's light shines out afar,
And it keeps me from dismaying,
When the clouds are ink above us,
And the sea runs white with foam.
In a cot in Connemara,
There's a wife and wee ones praying,
To the One who walked the waters once,
To bring us safely home.

Follow Me Up to Carlow

Patrick Joseph McCall (1861-1919)

Lift, MacCahir Óg, your face,
Brooding o'er the old disgrace,
That black FitzWilliam stormed your place,
Drove you to the Fern,
Grey said victory was sure,
Soon the firebrand he'd secure;
Until he met at Glenmalure,
With Fiach MacHugh O'Byrne.

Chorus
Curse and swear Lord Kildare,
Fiach will do what Fiach will dare.
Now FitzWilliam, have a care.
Fallen is your star, low.
Up with halberd out with sword.
On we'll go for by the lord.
Fiach MacHugh has given the word,
Follow me up to Carlow.

See the swords of Glen Imaal,
Flashing o'er the English Pale,
See all the children of the Gael,
Beneath O'Byrne's banners.
Rooster of the fighting stock,
Would you let a Saxon cock
Crow out upon an Irish rock,
Fly up and teach him manners.

From Tassagart to Clonmore,
There flows a stream of Saxon gore,
Oh, great is Rory Óg O'More,
At sending loons to Hades.
White is sick and Lane is fled,
Now for black FitzWilliam's head,
We'll send it over, dripping red,
To Queen Liza and her ladies.

The Ould Lammas Fair

John MacAuley (fl. 1920s)

At the ould Lammas fair in Ballycastle long ago,
I met a little colleen, who set my heart aglow;
She was smiing at her daddy buying lambs from Paddy Roe,
At the ould Lammas fair in Ballycastle, O!
Sure I saw her home that night,
When the moon was shining bright,
From the ould Lammas Fair in Ballycastle, O!

Chorus
At the ould Lammas fair, boys, were you ever there?
Were you ever at the fair in Ballycastle, O?
Did you treat your Mary Ann to dulse and yellow man,
At the ould Lammas fair at Ballycastle, O!

In Flanders field afar while resting from the war,
We drank bonne santé to the Flemish lassies, O;
But the scene that haunts my memory is kissing Mary Ann,
Her pouting lips all sticky from eating yellow man,
As we crossed the silver Margey and strolled across the strand
From the ould Lammas fair at Ballycastle, O!

There's a neat little cabin on the slopes of ould Knocklade.
It's lit by love and sunshine where the heather honey's made
By the bees ever humming, and our childers' joyous call
Resounds across the valley when the shadows fall.
I take my fiddle down and my Mary smiling there,
Brings back a happy memory of the Lammas fair.

Biddy Mulligan

Seamus Kavanagh (d. 1964)

(adapted from an earlier version by W.S. North)

I'm a buxom fine widow; I live in a spot,
In Dublin, they call it the Coombe.
My shops and my stalls are laid out on the street,
And my palace consists of one room.
I sell apples and oranges, nuts and split peas,
Bananas and sugar-stick sweet.
On Saturday night I sell second-hand clothes
From the floor of my stall on the street.

Chorus
You may travel from Clare,
To the County Kildare,
From Francis Street on to Macroom,
But where would you see
A fine widow like me?
Biddy Mulligan, the pride of the Coombe.

I sell fish on a Friday, spread out on a board,
The finest you'd find in the sea.
But the best is my herrings, fine Dublin Bay herrings;
There's herrings for dinner today!
I have a son Mick and he's great on the flute.
He plays in the Longford Street band,
It would do your heart good to see him march out,
On a Sunday for Dollymount Strand.

In the park on a Sunday I make quite a dash,
The neighbours look on with surprise.
With my Aberdeen shawlie thrown over my head,
I dazzle the sight of their eyes.
At Patrick Street corner for sixty-four years,
I've stood and no one can deny,
That while I stood there no person could dare,
To say black was the white of my eye.

Cruacha Glas' na hÉireann

Amhrán na bhFiann

Peadar Kearney (1883-1942)/Liam Ó Rinn (1888-1943)

Sinne Fianna Fáil,
Atá fé gheall ag Éirinn,
Buíon dár slua tar túinn do ráinig chughainn,
Fé mhóid bheith saor,
Sean-tír ár sinnsear feasta
Ní fhágfar fén tíorán ná fé'n tráil;
Anocht a théim sa bhearna baoil,
Le gean ar Ghaeil chun báis nó saoil,
Le gunnaí scréach: fé lamhach na bpiléar.
Seo libh canaíg' amhrán na bhFiann.

Seo dhibh a cháirde duan óglaigh,
Caithréimeach, bríomhar, ceolmhar.
Ár dtinte cnámh go buacach táid,
'S an spéir go mín réaltógach.
Is fonnmhar faobhrach sinn chun gleo,
'S go tiúnmhar glé roimh thíocht don ló,
Fé chiúnas caomh na hoíche ar seol,
Seo libh, canaíg' amhrán na bhFiann.

Éamann an Chnoic

Anon

'Cé hé sin amuigh ar mhaoilinn an chnoic,
Ag síorchur mo chodladh amú orm?'
'Tá Éamann an Chnoic an péarla breá fir,
'Sé ag iarraidh dul ina dhúiche.'
'A Rí 's a chuid, cad a dhéanfas mé riot,
Mara dtóga mé binn de mo ghúna,
Ach tá an oíche seo fliuch is é ag síobadh anoir,
Is bh'féidir go ndéanfaí ár bplúchadh.'

'Is fada mise amugh faoi shneachta agus faoi shioc,
Is gan dánacht agam ar éinne,
Mo sheisreach gan scor, mo bhranar gan cur,
Is gan iad agam ar aon chor.
Nil caraid agam, is danaid liom sin,
Do ghlacfadh mé moch ná déanach,
Is go gcaithfidh mé dul thar farraige soir,
Ós ann nach bhfuil mo ghaolta.'

An Spailpín Fánach

Anon

Im spailpín fánach atáim le fada,
Ag seasamh ar mo shláinte,
Ag siúl na drúchta go moch ar maidin,
'S ag bailiú galair ráithe,
Ach glacfad *fees* ó rí na *gcroppies*,
Cleith is píc chun sáite,
Is go brách arís ní ghlaofar m'ainm,
Sa tír seo, an spailpín fánach.

Ba mhinic mo thriall go Cluain Geal Meala,
'S as san go Tiobrad Árainn;
I gCarraig na Siúire thíos do ghearrainn,
Cúrsa leathan láidir;
I gCallainn go dlúth 's mo shúiste im ghlaic,
Ag dul chun tosaigh ceard leo,
'S nuair a théim go Dúrlas 's é siúd bhíonn agam,
'Sin chughaibh an spailpín fánach.'

Go deo deo arís ní raghad go Caiseal,
Ag díol ná ag reic mo shláinte,
Ná ar mharagadh na saoire im shuí cois balla,
Im scaoinse ar leataoibh sráide,
Bodairí na tíre ag teacht ar a gcapaill,
Á fhiafraí an bhfuilim híreálta,
'Téanam chun siúil, tá an cúrsa fada.'
Siud siúl ar an spailpín fánach.

Mó shlán beo siar chun dúiche m'athar,
Agus chun an oileáin ghrámhair,
Is chun buachaillí na Cúlach os díobh nár mheata,
In aimsir chasta an ghárda,
Ach anois ó táimse im chaonaí dealamh,
I measc na ndúthaí fáin seo,
'Sé is é chumha mo chroí mar fuaireas de ghairm,
Bheith riamh im spailpín fánach.

Is ró-bhreá is cuimhin liom mo dhaoine bheith sealad,
Thiar 'ge Droichead Gháile,
Fá bhuaibh, fá chaoraigh, fá laonna geala,
Agus capaill ann le háireamh,
Dob é toil Chríost é gur cuireadh sinn astu,
'S go ndeachamar i leath ár sláinte,
'S gurbh é bhris mo chroí i ngach tír dá dtagainn,
'Call here, you spailpín fánach.'

Dá dtigeadh an Francach anall thar caladh,
'S a champaí daingean láidir,
Is Boc Ó Gráda chughainn abhaile,
Is Tadhg bocht fial Ó Dálaigh;
Bheadh *barracks* an rí again á leagadh,
Agus Yeos go leor á gcarnadh,
Bheadh clanna Gall gach am á dtreascairt –
Sin cabhair ag an spailpín fánach.

Caoineadh Chill Chais

Anon

Kilcash Castle, at the foot of Sliabh na mBan near Carrick-on-Suir in County Tipperary, belonged to the Butler family in the early eighteenth century.

Cad a dhéanfaimíd feasta gan adhmad?
Ta deireadh na gcoillte ar lár,
Níl trácht ar Cill Chais ná ar a teaghlach,
Is ni chluinfear a cling go brach.
An áit úd ina gconaíodh an deighbhean,
Fuair gradam is meidhir thar mhná,
Bhiodh iarlaí ag tarraingt thar toinn ann,
Is an tAifreann binn á rá.

Ni chluinim fuaim lachan na gé ann,
Na fiolair ag éamh cois cuain,
Ni fiú na mbeacha chun saothair,
'Thabharfadh mil agus céir don tslúa.
Níl ceol binn milis na n-éan ann,
Le hamharc an lae a dhul uainn,
Na an chuaichín i mbarra na gcraobh ann,
Ó 's í a chuirfeadh an saol chun suain.

Aicím ar Mhuire is ar Iosa,
Go dtaga sí arís chugainn slan,
Go mbeidh rince fada ag gabháil timpeall,
Ceol veidhlín is tinte cnámh.
Go dtógtar an baile seo ár sinsear,
Cill Chais bhreá arís go hard,
Is go bráth no go dtiocfaidh an dile,
Ná feicfear í arís ar lár.

from Cáit Ní Dhuibhir

Anon

Although probably composed at the beginning of the 19th century, this song draws on an earlier tradition of the aisling, *the* spéirbhean *herself and the names 'Cáit Ní Dhuibhir' and 'Fodla' representing Ireland.*

Tráthnóinín beag déanach 's mo thréada agam á gcur ón síon,
Ar leataoibh chnoic im aonar 's ba ghléasta do bhí mo phíob,
Bhí an ceol ba bhinne ab fhéidir ag éanlaith 's gach nóta fíor,
'S do réir mar thuigeas féin iad, beidh Éire 'ge Cáit Ní Dhuibhir.

Tá liosacháinín aerach ar an dtaobh seo, 'ge ceann mo thí,
'S is moch gach maidin ghréine a bhíonn an spéirbhean ann romham
    'na suí;
Tá leabhar aici den Ghaelainn is beagáinín den Bhéarla tríd,
'Sé scríofa i mbun gach véarsa ann go mbeidh Éire 'ge Cáit ní Dhuibhir.

Tá míle dath 'na clóicín 's a bróigín ar dhath an fhraoigh,
Is gúna den bhfaisean nua uirthi den tsórt a bhíonn ar 'níon an rí,
'A chumainn chroi 's a stóir dhíl, suigh go fóillín 's ní neosad puinn,
Ach go raghainnse arís im óige dá mbeadh Fódla 'ge Cáit Ní Dhuibhir.'

Táimse Im' Chodladh

Anon

Another Munster aisling: *the tune is a haunting slow air.*

Tráthnóinín déanach i gcéin cois leasa dom,
Táimse im' chodhladh is ná dúistear mé.
Sea dhearcas lem' thaobh an spéirbhean mhaisiúil,
Táimse im' chodhladh is ná dúistear mé.

Ba bhachallach péarlach dréimreach barrachas,
A carnfholt craobhach ag titim léi ar bhaillechrith
'S í ag caitheamh na saighead trím thaobh do chealg mé,
Táimse im' chodhladh is ná dúistear mé.

'Is mo bhuachaillin óg a tógadh go ceannasach.'
Táimse im' chodhladh is ná dúistear mé,
'Do cuireadh le foirneart anonn thar farraige.'
Táimse im' chodhladh is ná dúistear mé.

'Go bhfeicfead an lá a mbeidh ár ar Shasanaigh,
Ughaim ar a ndroim is iad ag treabhadh is ag branar dúinn,
Gan mise a bheith ann mura dtéanam an maide leo.'
Táimse im' chodhladh is ná dúistear mé.

Dóchas Linn Naomh Pádraig

Anon

Dóchas linn Naomh Pádraig,
Aspal mór na hÉireann,
Ainm oirearc gléigeal,
Solas mór an tsaoil é.
'Sé do chlaoi na draíothe
Croíthe dúra gan aon mhaith
D'ísligh dream an díómais
Tré neart Dé ár dtréan-fhlaith.

Sléibhte, gleannta máighe,
'S bailte mór' na hÉireann,
Ghlan sé iad go deo dúinn,
Míle glóir dár naomh dhil.
Iarraimíd ort, a Phádraig,
Guí orainne Gaela,
Dia linn ló 'gus oíche,
'S Pádraig aspal Éireann.

Cruacha na hÉireann

Anon

Tá an samhradh ag sileadh a shéada,
Inniu ar fud Oileán na Naomh.
Tá an ghrian ag soilsiú go glégeal,
'S ag líonadh le haoibhneas an tír.
Ó, is minic mé 'smaointiú ar filleadh,
Ar ais annsar cáirde mó chléibh;
I measc subhailcí sona mo chine,
'Na gcónaí fé chruacha na hÉireann.

Curfá
Cruacha glas' na hÉireann,
'Lonnrú measc coillte craoibh.
Ó a charaid nach méanair,
Sinne fé dheireadh ag filleadh thar sáile.
Gaotha grinn dár seoladh,
Luascadh ar dhroim na mara;
Ó, ní fada go mbeimíd slán,
Sa bhaile fé chruacha na hÉireann

Is fada an lá é ó d'fhágamar,
Ár mbaile 's ár muintir i mbrón,
Ag dréim lenár bpócaí a líonadh,
Thar sáile le hairgead is ór.
Ó nach cuma má táimid ag filleadh,
Gan pingin inár bpócaí faraoir,
Tá an sláinte go fóill inár gcnámha,
Ag filleadh go cruacha na hÉireann.

Trasna na dTonnta

Anon

Curfá
Trasna na dtonnta 'dul siar, 'dul siar!
Slán leis an uaigneas is slán leis an gcian!
Geal é mo chroí agus geal í an ghrian!
Geal bheith ag filleadh go hÉirinn!

Chonac mo dhóthain de thíortha i gcéin,
Ór agus airgead, saibhreas an tsaoil.
Éiríonn an croí 'nam le breacadh gach lae,
'S mé 'g druidim le dúthaigh mo mhuintir'.

Muintir an iarthair 's iad cairde mo chroí;
Fáilte 'gus fiche beidh romham ar gach taobh;
Ar fhágaint an tsaoil seo 'sea guím ar an Rí:
Gur leosan a shínfear i gcré mé.

Fáinne Geal an Lae

Anon

Maidin moch do ghabhas amach,
Ar bhruach Locha Léin,
An samhradh 'teacht 's an chraobh len 'ais,
Is lonrach te ón ngréin,
Ar thaisteal dom trí bhailte poirt is bánta míne réidhe,
Cé a gheobhainn le m'ais ach an chúileann deas,
Le fáinne geal an lae.

Ní raibh bróg ná stoca, caidhp ná clóc,
Ar mo stóirín óg ón spéir,
Ach folt fionn órga síos go troigh,
Ag fás go barr an fhéir.
Bhí calán crúite aici ina glaic,
'S ar dhrúcht ba dheas a scéimh,
Do rug barr gean ar Bhéineas deas,
Le fáinne geal an lae.

Do shuigh an bhrídeog síos le m'ais,
Ar bhinse glas den bhféar,
Ag magadh léi, bhíos dá maíomh go pras,
Mar mhnaoi nach scarfainn léi.
'Sé dúirt sí liomsa, 'Imigh uaim,
Is scaoil ar siúl mé, a réic.'
Sin iad aneas na soilse ag teacht.
Le fáinne geal an lae.

from Mac an Cheannaí

Aogán Ó Rathaile (1670-1726)

The earliest and probably the finest of the *aisling* poems of the 18th
century, written about 1700.

Aisling ghéar do dhearcas féin,
Ar leaba 's mé go lagbhríoch.
An ainnir séimh darbh ainm Éire,
Ag teacht im ghaor ag marcaíocht,
A súile glas, a cúl tiubh casta, a com ba gheal 's a mailí,
Dhá maíomh go raibh ag tíócht na gar,
A díogras, mac an Cheannaí.

A beol ba bhinn, a glór ba chaoin,
Is ró-shearc linn an cailín,
Céile Bhriain dár ghéill an Fhiann,
Mo léirchreach dhian a haicíd:
Fá shiústibh Gall dá brú go teann,
Mo chúileann tseang 'm bhean ghaoil;
Beidh sí 'na spreas, an rí-bhean deas,
go bhfilllfidh Mac an Cheannaí.

...

Do-bheir siúl ó dheas gach la fá seach,
Ar thráigh na mbarc an cailín,
Is súil deas soir go dlúth thar muir,
Mo chumha anois a haicíd,
A súile siar ag súil le Dia,
Tar tonntaibh fiara gainmhe;
Cloíte lag beidh sí gan phreab,
Go bhfillfidh Mac an Cheannaí.

from Bímse Buan ar Buairt Gach Ló

Seán Clárach Mac Domhnaill?(1691-1754)

Bímse buan ar buairt gach ló,
Ag caoi go cruaidh 's ag tuar na ndeór,
Mar scaoileadh uaim an buachaill beo,
'S ná ríomhthar tuairisc uaidh, mo bhrón.

Curfá
Is é mo laoch, mo ghille mear,
Is é mo Shaesar, gille mear,
Suan ná séan ní bhfuaireas féin,
Ó chuaigh i gcéin mo gille mear.

Ní haoibhinn cuach ba suairc' ar nóin,
Táid fíorchoin uaisle ar uatha spóirt,
Táid saoithe 's suadha i mbuairt 's i mbrón,
Ó scaoileadh uainn an buachaill beo.

Marcach uasal uaibhreach óg,
Gas gan ghruaim i suairce snó,
Glac is luaimneach luath i ngleo,
At teascadh an tsluaigh 's ag tuargain treon.

from Slán le Croma

Aindrias Mac Craith (1710-1790)

This lament is more popularly known as 'Slán le Máighe', the River
Maigue mentioned in the first stanza.

Slán is céad ón dtaobhsa uaim,
Cois Mháighe na gcaor, na gcraobh, 's na gcruach,
Na stair, na séad, na saor, na slua,
Na ndán, na ndréacht, na dtréan gan ghruaim.

Curfá
Och! Ochón! is breoite mise,
Gan chuid, gan chóir, gan chóip, gan chiste,
Gan sult, gan seoid, gan spórt, gan spionnadh
Ó seoladh mé chun uaignis.

Slán go héag dá saoirfhir suairc',
Dá dáimh, dá héigs', dá cléir, dá suaidh,
Dom chairde chléibh gan chlaoin gan chluain,
Gan cháim gan chaon, gan chraos, gan chruas.

Slán dá n-éis dá béithe uaim,
Dá mná go léir, dá séimh, dá snua,
Dá gcáil, dá gcéill, dá gcéim, dá gcuaird,
Dá bpráisc, dá bplé, dá méin, dá mbua.

from Bánchnoic Éireann Ó

Donncha Rua Mac Conmara? (1715-1810)

Beir beannacht óm chroí go tír na hÉireann,
Bánchnoic Éireann Ó,
Chun a maireann de shíolrach Ír is Éibhir,
Ar bhánchnoic Éireann Ó,
An áit úd 'narbh aoibhinn binnghuth éan,
Mar shnámhchruit chaoin ag caoineadh Gael;
'Sé mo chás bheith míle míle i gcéin,
Ó bhánchnoic Éireann Ó.

Bíonn barra slim ar chaoinchnoic Éireann,
Bánchnoic Éireann Ó,
'S is fearra ná an tír seo díogha gach sléibhe ann,
Bánchnoic Éireann Ó,
Is ard na coillte 's is díreach réidh,
'S a mbláth mar aol ar mhaoilinn géag –
Ta grá dem chroí im intinn féin,
Do bhánchnoic Éireann Ó.

Tá gasra líonmhar i dtír na hÉireann,
Bánchnoic Éireann Ó,
D'fheara-choin ghroí ná cloífeadh céadta.
Ar bhánchnoic Éireann Ó,
M'atuirse croí 's mo chaoineadh géar,
Iad ag Galla-phoic thíos fá ghreim, mo léan!
'S a mbuailte á roinnt fá chíos go daor,
Bánchnoic Éireann Ó.

Cill Aodáin

Antaine Ó Raifteirí (1779-1835)

Anois teacht an Earraigh beidh an lá 'dúl chun shíneadh,
Is tar eis na féile Bríde, ardóigh mé mo sheol.
Ó chuir mé im' cheann é ní stopfaidh mé choíche,
Go seasfaidh mé thíos i lár Chontae Mhaigh Eo.
I gClár Chlainne Mhuiris a bheas mé an chéad oíche,
Is i mBalla taobh thíos de 's ea thosós mé ag ól,
Go Coillte Mách rachad go ndéanad cuairt mhíosa ann,
I bhfogas dhá mhíle do Bhéal an Átha Mhóir.

Fágaim le huachta go n-éiríonn mo chroí-se,
Mar ardaíos an ghaoth nó mar scaipeas an ceo,
Nuair a smaoiním ar Chearra nó ar Bhalla taobh thíos de,
Ar Sceach an dá Mhíle 's ar phlánaí Mhaigh Eo.
Cill Aodáin an baile a bhfásann gach ní ann,
Tá sméara 's sú craobh' ann is meas de gach sórt,
Is dá mbéinnse i mo sheasamh i gceartlár mo dhaoine
D'éirodh an aois díom is bheinn arís óg.

Mise Raifteirí

Seán Ó Ceallagh (fl. 1880)

Mise Raifteírí an file, lán dóchais is grá,
Le súile gan solas, ciúineas gan crá,
'Dul síar ar m'aistear le solas mo chroí,
Fann agus tuirseach go deireadh mo shlí;
Tá mé anois lem aghaidh ar bhalla,
'Seinm cheoil do phócaí falamh'.

Óró 'Sé do Bheatha 'Bhaile

Pádraic Mac Piarais (1879-1916)

Curfá
Óró 'sé do bheatha 'bhaile,
Óró 'sé do bheatha 'bhaile,
Óró 'sé do bheatha 'bhaile,
Anois ar theacht an tsamhraidh!

Sé do bheatha a bhean ba léanmhar,
B'é ár gcreach tú bheith i ngéibhinn,
Do dhúiche bhreá i seilbh méirleach,
Is tú díolta leis na Gallaibh!

Tá Gráinne Mhaol ag teacht thar sáile,
Óglaigh armtha léi mar gharda,
Gaeil iad féin is ní Gaill ná Spáinnigh.
Is cuirfidh siad ruaig ar Ghallaibh.

A bhuí le Rí na bhFeart go bhfeiceann,
Mura mbím beo ina dhiaidh ach seachtain,
Gráinne Mhaol agus míle gaiscíoch.
Ag fógairt fáin ar Ghallaibh!

Amhrán Dóchais

Osborn Bergin (1873-1950)

Slán go deo le brón is buairt,
Slán gan mhoill dár gcaoineadh dhuairc;
Canaim laoithe dóchais
I dteanga bhinn na Fódla,
'Gus seasaimís go beomhar
Os comhair an tsaoil.
Ó, canaim laoithe dóchais
I dteanga bhinn na Fódla,
'Gus seasaimis go beomhar
Os comhair an tsaoil.

Clanna Gael faoi réim gan ruaig!
Beidh siad saor is béarfaidh bua.
Leanfaimíd an lóchrann
Do las ár sinsir romhainn,
Is ní heagal linn go bhfeofaidh
A gcró 'nár ndiaidh.
Ó, leanfaimíd an lóchrann
Do las ár sinsir romhainn,
Is ní heagal linn go bhfeofaidh
A gcró 'nár ndiaidh,

Biographical Index of Poets

Alexander, Cecil Frances (1818–95) was born in Dublin and went to live in Derry when her clergyman husband was ordained Bishop of Derry and Raphoe. Her three best-known hymns, 'All Things Bright and Beautiful', 'Once in Royal David's City' and 'There Is a Green Hill Far Away', were published in *Hymns for Little Children* in 1848.

Allingham, William (1824–89) was born in Ballyshannon, County Donegal, and worked as a customs officer in different posts in Ireland until he settled in England in 1863. *Poems* (1850) contains most of his best work.

Bergin, Osborn (1873-1950 was born in Cork and educated in Queen's College (now UCC) and Berlin. A Celtic scholar and expert in linguistics, he later taught in University College, Dublin.

Blacker, William (1777–1855) was born in Carrickblacker, near Portadown, County Armagh, the son of a yeoman captain, and educated in TCD. Tradition places him at the Battle of the Diamond (1795) and much of his life was spent in support of all things Orange: he held the rank of colonel in the militia.

Boucicault, Dion (1820–90) was born in Dublin. He attended London University but left after a year to go on the stage. He wrote a hundred and fifty plays, the most notable being three Irish comic melodramas, *The Colleen Bawn*, *Arrah na Pogue* and *The Shaughraun*. He died in New York.

Brayton, Teresa (1868-1943) was born Teresa Boylan near Kilcock, County Kildare, in 1868. She emigrated to America in 1895 and became well known in Irish-American circles, publishing three collections of poetry treating of exile, nationalism and religion. She returned permanently to Ireland in 1932.

Burrows, Robert (1756–1841) was born in Dublin, educated in TCD and became a Fellow there in 1782. Later he was consecrated Dean of Cork. He was a friend of John Philpot Curran and the other 'Monks of the Screw', who enjoyed wit and liquor in equal measure. Though he denied the authorship of the remarkable 'The Night before Larry Was Stretched', no one believed him.

Carleton, William (1794–1869) was born to a family of Irish-speaking farmers at Prillisk in the Clogher valley of County Tyrone. Although he lived for much of his life in Dublin, he wrote several novels about the Tyrone people he knew best, as well as the largely autobiographical *Traits and Stories of the Irish Peasantry*.

Carlin, Francis (1881–1941) was born James Francis Carlin MacDonnell in Long Island, New York. He published a book, *The Cairn of Stars*, in 1920 as by Francis Carlin, the name of his grandfather, who was a weaver and local rhymer in that part of Tyrone where his popular poem 'A Ballad of Douglas Bridge' is set. Nothing else of his life is known.

Casey, John Keegan (1846–70) was born near Mullingar, County Westmeath, the son of a teacher. He taught school and later worked as a clerk before his arrest as a Fenian after the failed rising of 1867. 'The Rising of the Moon', which gave Lady Gregory the title for her most famous play, was written when he was fifteen.

Cherry, Andrew (1762–1812) was the son of a Limerick bookseller who became an actor, playwright and manager of the Theatre Royal, Drury Lane, London, in 1802. He died in poverty in Monmouth.

Connolly, Luke Aylmer (*c.* 1786–1833) Little is known of him except that he was a clergyman and as well as the 'The Enchanted Isle', a favourite anthology piece, published *Irish Tales of Wonder* in 1813.

Curran, John Philpot (1750–1817) was born in Newmarket, County Cork. A lawyer, patriot and orator, he was the father of Robert Emmet's love, Sarah Curran. During his career at the Bar he ably defended many united Irishmen and as an MP he strongly opposed the Act of Union

Davis, Thomas (1814–45) was born in Mallow, County Cork, but lived in Dublin for most of his short life. Educated in TCD, he was called to the bar in 1838. He was one of the founders of *The Nation*, the organ of the Young Ireland movement, and is remembered for stirring ballads that recalled Ireland's former glories. He died of scarlatina.

de Vere, Aubrey (1814-1902) was the son of Sir Aubrey de Vere (1788–1846) of Curragh Chase, County Limerick. He was educated in TCD and through his father became friendly with most of the mid-Victorian poetic establishment, including Tennyson. His poetry had historical, mythological and (after his conversion to Catholicism) religious themes.

Drennan, William (1754–1820) was born in Belfast and became a doctor, settling to a practice in Dublin in 1789. He joined the United Irishmen and wrote their original prospectus. Arrested in 1794, he was acquitted of treason, ably defended by John Philpot Curran, and played no further part in politics.

Dufferin, Lady (1807–67) Helen Sheridan, granddaughter of the dramatist Richard Brinsley Sheridan, grew up in South Africa. She married Captain Blackwood, who succeeded to the barony of Dufferin in 1839.

Fahy, Francis (1854-1935) was born in Kinvara, County Galway, but spent all his working life as a civil servant in London. He became involved in Irish cultural and literary organisations and was president of Conradh na Gaeilge in the city from 1896 to 1908.

Ferguson, Samuel (1810–86) was born in Belfast and educated in TCD, where he became a nationalist under the influence of Thomas Davis: his poems, some of them versions of Irish lyrics, were strongly influenced by mythology and the rhythm and cadence of the Irish language. He became Deputy Keeper of Public

Records and had a literary salon at his home in Dublin.

French, Percy (1854–1920) was born in Cloonyquin, County Roscommon, and after a leisurely career in TCD finally emerged to become 'Inspector of Drains', in County Cavan, as one of his songs recalls, . Even as a student he had begun to write the mainly comic songs for which he is noted. He was also a talented watercolourist.

Goldsmith, Oliver (1724–72) was born in Pallas, County Longford, the son of an Anglican curate. He was educated in Athlone and attended TCD, becoming a teacher and hack in London and later a successful playwright. Though rather the butt of Dr Johnson's Club, he was loved for his sweet nature and valued for the excellence of his essays, although infamous for his fecklessness.

Graves, Alfred Perceval (1846–1931) was born in Dublin. He was educated in TCD and became a schools inspector in England. He compiled several anthologies of Irish poetry and wrote popular lyrics to traditional Irish tunes.

Gregory, Pádraic (1886–1962) was born in Belfast and became a successful ecclesiastical architect. He published several books of ballads, simple tangible pieces that were often set pieces at *feiseanna*.

Griffin, Gerald (1803-40) was born and educated in Limerick. He is famous as the author of *The Collegians* (1829), a novel of passion and murder, which became very popular and provided Boucicault with the material for his first success, *The Colleen Bawn.* (1860).

Hopper, Nora (1871–1906) was born in Exeter, the daughter of an army captain. As well as poetry she wrote the libretto for the opera, *The Sea Swan*, in 1903.

Hull, Eleanor (1860–1935) was born in Manchester and educated in Alexandra College after her family moved to Dublin. She was among the founders of the Irish Texts Society and published several valuable books on folklore and mythology, as well as translations of Irish poems.

Ingram, John Kells (1823–1907) was born near Pettigo, County Donegal, and educated in Newry and TCD, where he eventually held the Chair of Greek. 'The Memory of the Dead' was published anonymously in *The Nation* in April 1843, when Ingram was still a student.

Joyce, Robert Dwyer (1830–83) was born in Glenosheen, County Limerick and educated in local hedge schools. He graduated as a doctor from Queen's College, Cork, in 1865, having already published a collection of verse, *Ballads, Romances and Songs* (1861). A known Fenian supporter, he lived for most of his life in the US.

Kavanagh, Seamus (d. 1964) was born in County Wexford and was active in the 1916 Rising and the War of Independence. He is remembered as the author of many popular songs.

Kearney, Peadar (1883-1942) was born in Dublin and educated at CBS, Marino. In 1911 he published 'The Soldier's Song' in *Irish Freedom* and it was adopted as a war song by the IRA and eventually as the national anthem for the new state, translated into Irish by Liam Ó Rinn.

Keegan, John (1809-49) was born in Queen's County (Laois) and educated at a local hedge school. He contributed verse to the available periodicals, *The Nation*, *The Irish Penny Journal* and *The Dublin University Magazine*. He died of cholera in Dublin.

Kenneally, William (1828-76) was born in Cloyne, County Cork. He contributed verse to periodicals under the pseudonym 'William of Munster': 'The Moon behind the Hill' was published in *The Nation* in 1856. He was a newspaper editor and spent much of his life in Kilkenny.

Kettle, Thomas (1880-1916) was born in Dublin and educated at Clongowes and UCD. He joined the Royal Dublin Fusiliers and after the Rising of 1916 volunteered for service in Belgium. His essays were published in *The Day's Burden* (1910) and his famous sonnet 'To My Daughter Betty, the Gift of God' was written shortly before his death at Ginchy on the Somme.

Kickham, Charles Joseph (1828–1882) was born near Mullinahone, County Tipperary, and made deaf at the age of thirteen by an accident with gunpowder. He was a strong supporter of Young Ireland and became a Fenian in 1860, editing the movement's newspaper, *The Irish People*. He was arrested in 1865 after the short-lived Fenian Rising but served only four years of his fourteen-year sentence because of poor health. He survived for a further dozen years, publishing his famous romance, *Knocknagow*, in 1879.

Lever, Charles (1805–72) was born in Dublin and educated in TCD and the Royal College of Surgeons. In 1832 he was appointed dispensary doctor in Portstewart, County Derry. With his military novels he established a genre of popular comic fiction describing the (mainly romantic) adventures of young subalterns in Ireland. From 1839 he lived in Europe, working as a doctor and a writer.

Locke, John (1847–89) was born near Callan, County Kilkenny, and became involved with Fenianism, writing for the movement's *Irish People* newspaper while still in his teens. After serving a short jail sentence he moved to Manchester, thence to the US. He published novels and short stories as well as poetry.

Lover, Samuel (1797–1868) was born in Dublin and trained as a painter, specialising in seascapes and miniatures. A competent singer, he began writing songs and stories for the Dublin magazines, from one of which grew the popular play *Rory O'More*. He moved to London in 1833 and became a well-known figure in the literary circles of the capital. He wrote three hundred songs in all and died in St Helier, Jersey.

MacAuley John Henry (d. 1937) was a local shopkeeper and wood carver in Ballycastle, County Antrim, a town he made famous by his ballad, 'The Ould Lammas Fair'. He was also a skilled fiddler.

McBurney, William (1844–92) was born in County Down in 1844. He emigrated to the US and worked there as a journalist. His work was published in *The Nation*.

McCall Patrick Joseph (1861–1919) was born in Dublin to a father from the Carlow-Wexford border who collected traditional songs, and educated at the Royal University. Later he kept a pub. He is remembered for his ballads of 1798, written for the centenary celebrations, notably 'Boolavogue' and 'Kelly from Killane'.

McCann, Michael Joseph (1824–83) was born in Galway and taught in St Jarlath's, the junior seminary in Tuam. One of the many poets who contributed to *The Nation*, he later went to London and became a journalist and editor of the short-lived periodical, *The Harp*.

MacCarthy, Denis Florence (1817–82) was born in Dublin and educated in Maynooth. His ballads and poems were published in *The Nation* and *Dublin University Magazine* and he was the first professor of English in the Catholic University.

Mac Conmara, Donncha Rua (1715-1810) was (it is thought) born in County Clare and spent much of his life teaching in County Waterford. One of his best-known poems, 'Eachtra Ghiolla an Amaráin', is a description of an emigrant's trip to Newfoundland, a trip he himself may have made in about 1745.

Mac Craith, Aindrias (1710-90) was born somewhere in the River Maigue area in County Limerick. He was a teacher, for a time a peddler, by tradition a womaniser and one of the poets of the Maigue school ('filí na Máighe').

Mac Domhnaill, Seán Clárach (1691-1754) was born near Charleville to a prosperous farming family and received a good classical education locally. His poetic output included patriotic works lamenting the misfortunes of the Stuarts, laments and satires; one of these, 'Taiscidh a Chlocha', on the death of local landlord, Colonel Dawson, caused such offence that the poet had to flee his home for a time.

Mac Piarais, Pádraic *see* **Pearse, Pádraic**

MacDonagh, Thomas (1878–1916) was born in Cloughjordan, County Tipperary, and educated at Rockwell College and the Royal University, becoming a lecturer in English. He joined the IRB in 1913 and, as one of the signatories of the 1916 Proclamation, was executed on 3 May. His poetry was strongly influenced by his Catholicism and by the literary revival.

Maedar, James Gaspard (1809–76) was born in Ireland in 1809 and began a musical career of composition and performance in London. He married the actress Clara Fisher and they became significant figures in New York musical circles in 1827. He is now remembered only for the nostalgic 'Teddy O'Neale'.

Mangan, James Clarence (1803–49) was born in Dublin. His later, strongly nationalistic poetry, was published in *The Nation* and his work admired by W.B. Yeats. Addicted to alcohol and opium, isolated and eccentric, Mangan became the very model of a *poète maudit*, and died of cholera in the epidemic of 1849.

Meyer, Kuno (1859–1919) was born in Hamburg and while studying in Liverpool became interested in Celtic languages. A key figure in the Irish revival movement, he became Professor of Celtic in Berlin.

Moore, Thomas (1779–1852) was born in Aungier Street in Dublin. He entered TCD in 1794 and became a close friend of Robert Emmet. He was intended for the law but patronage, a fine tenor voice and a genuine skill with light verse provided an agreeable London life. He lives on in his *Irish Melodies* and a few other song-lyrics.

Mulchinock, William (1820–64) was born in Tralee, County Kerry, in 1822. A supporter of Daniel O'Connell, he had to flee the country after an affray for which he was held responsible. He returned to Ireland in 1849.

Ó Ceallagh, Seán (*fl.* 1880) was born in Loughrea, County Galway and emigrated to the US. He lived in Oswego in New York State in the 1880s and became involved in the Irish language movement. He claimed (improbably) to have heard 'Mise Raifteirí' from Raifteirí himself.

Ó Raifteirí, Antaine (1779-1835) was born in Kiledan near Kiltimagh in County Mayo. As a small child he became blind as a result of contracting smallpox. He made his living by playing the fiddle and reciting songs and poems in the more prosperous homes in Galway and Mayo.

Ó Rathaile, Aogán (1670-1726) was born at Screathan a' Mhíl in the Sliabha Luachra district of east Kerry. He belonged to a family of small landowners that owed fealty to the native chieftains, the MacCarthys, who were supplanted by the Jacobite Brownes, and much of his poetry is the mournful cry of the client who fell with the fall of his master. Regarded as the greatest of Irish-language poets, he died in poverty near Dingle.

Ó Rinn, Liam (1888–1943) was involved in drafting the Irish versions both of the 1922 Constitution and of the 1937 Constitution. He worked as a translator for the Houses of the Oireachtas in Dublin until his death.

O'Keefe, John (1747–1833) was born in Dublin and began a career as an artist but gave it up to join the Smock Alley theatre company in 1767. He spent the next dozen years as an actor, mainly on tour In all he wrote sixty-eight theatrical pieces, mostly comic, and continued to dictate his work when totally blind in 1790, after twenty years of failing sight. His plays, including *Wild Oats*, were immensely popular in his time and have been successfully revived.

O'Shaughnessy, Arthur (1844–81) was born in London of Irish parents. He worked in the zoological department of the British Museum and published three volumes of poetry before he was thirty. His 'Ode' was set to music by Edward Elgar.

Orr, James (1770–1816) was known as 'The Bard of Ballycarry', his birthplace in County Antrim. He joined the United Irishmen in 1794 and took part in fighting in Antrim in 1798. He escaped capture, fleeing to America, but returned to Ballycarry under amnesty in 1802.

Patterson, Johnny (1840–89) was born near Feakle in County Clare. After five years in the army as a drummer boy, he joined Swallow's Circus and soon became a star turn as the 'Singing Irish Clown'. Using this persona and his own songs he had a very successful performing career in Ireland, Britain and America.

Pearse, Pádraic (1879–1916) was born in Dublin and educated in the Royal University and the King's Inns. He was one of the founders of the Irish Volunteers in 1913 and a member of the IRB. A signatory of the Proclamation of the Republic and President of the Provisional Government of Easter 1916, he was court-martialled and executed on 3 May of that year.

Petrie, Sir George (1789–1866) was born in Dublin and educated at the RDS art school. In 1833, he was employed by the Ordnance Survey and when funding for this work ceased in 1841 he continued to act as an advocate for Irish antiquities. To him must be given credit for the preservation of manuscripts like *The Annals of the Four Masters* and treasures such as the Cross of Cong.

Plunkett, Joseph Mary (1887–1916) was born in Dublin but had poor health and spent much time abroad. He was a signatory of the Proclamation of the Republic and was executed on 4 May 1916, having married Grace Gifford on the eve of his execution. His poetry is in two volumes, one posthumous.

Rolleston T.W. (1857–1920) was born in Shinrone, County Offaly, and educated in St Columba's College and TCD. He was founding editor of the *Dublin University Review*, compiler of *Poems and Ballads of Young Ireland* (1888) and secretary of the influential Irish Literary Society in London.

Rowe, Josephine V. (*fl.* 1910). Little is known of the author of the lyrics of 'Macushla', a song written in 1910 with music by Dermot MacMurrough. It owns it fame to its adoption as a concert encore by John McCormack and by many Irish tenors since.

'Shane, Elizabeth' (1877–1951) the pseudonym of Gertrude Hind, a rector's daughter who spent much of her life in west Donegal. She published several books of poetry set around the Rosses and Gweedore:

Shanly, Charles Dawson (1811–75) was born in Dublin and educated in TCD. He emigrated with his family to Canada, thence to New York. As well as being an artist and poet, he worked as a journalist and the editor of publications such as *Vanity Fair* and the *New York Saturday Press* in the 1850s and 1860s.

Sheridan, Richard Brinsley (1751–1816) was born in Dublin to parents involved in the theatre. The family moved to London when he was seven. A poet and playwright, he was for many years manager of the Drury Lane Theatre, which burned to the ground in 1809. His most famous plays are *The Rivals* and *The School for Scandal*.

Sullivan, Timothy Daniel (1827-1914) was born in Bantry, County Cork. He was editor-publisher of *The Nation*, Irish Party MP for various constituencies and the author of songs that achieved great popularity in Ireland and America. He edited numerous anthologies and published several volumes of poetry as well as a political memoir.

Swift, Jonathan (1667–1745) was born in Dublin of English parents and educated in Kilkenny College and TCD. Thwarted in his ambitions for ecclesiastical and political advancement, he grimly remained Dean of St Patrick's Cathedral in Dublin from 1714 until his death. A prose writer and satirist, he was a highly effective anti-government polemicist, although not out of any great regard for Ireland or the Irish.

Synge, J.M. (1871–1909) was born in Dublin and took a leisurely pass degree in TCD. Having learned Irish, he spent four summers (1899-1902) in the Aran Islands, especially Inis Meáin. He was the most significant dramatist of the literary revival and the author of sharply satiric verse, as well as a few love lyrics.

Tate, Nahum (1652– 1715) was born in Dublin, the son of a County Cavan Presbyterian minister. His own plays proving unpopular, he gave some of Shakespeare's tragedies happy endings. He wrote the libretto for Purcell's *Dido and Aeneas* (1689) and was named Poet Laureate in 1692.

Thackeray, William Makepeace (1811–63) was born in Calcutta. His wife was Irish and he first came to Ireland in 1840, commissioned by publishers Chapman and Hall to write *An Irish Sketchbook*, which was published pseudonymously in 1843. He stayed in an inn in Limavady in 1842 during his Irish journeying and wrote 'Peg of Limavaddy' in honour of the barmaid.

Tonna, Charlotte Elizabeth (1790–1846) was born in Norwich, the daughter of a clergyman, and came to live in Kilkenny with her first husband. She later married Lewis Tonna and went to live with him in Ulster. She wrote many religious tracts as 'Charlotte Elizabeth' and at least thirty novels. She was firmly anti-Catholic, regarding 'Popery as the curse of Ireland'.

Tynan, Katharine (1861–1931) was born in Dublin. An enthusiastic constitutional nationalist and feminist, she was mistress of a literary salon. She left Ireland for good in 1919, finding no common cause with Republicanism, and travelled extensively in Europe. She was a prolific poet, novelist and essayist.

Waddell, Helen (1889–1965) was born in Tokyo, the daughter of a Presbyterian minister, and educated at Victoria College, Belfast, QUB, and Somerville College, Oxford. A journalist, lecturer and broadcaster, her best-known work, *The Wandering Scholars* (1927), is a history of the medieval *vagantes*.

Waller, John Francis (1810–94) was born in Limerick and educated in TCD and the King's Inns. He was a contributor to and later editor of *Dublin University Magazine* and published several volumes of poetry, as well as writing popular songs.

Weatherly, Fred E. (1848–1929) was born in Somerset and educated in Oxford. A barrister, he wrote the lyrics for more than three thousand popular songs, including 'The Holy City' and 'Roses of Picardy'. 'Danny Boy' was played at his funeral in Bath Abbey.

Westendorf, Thomas P. (1848–1923), an American, was superintendent of Bartlett Training and Industrial School in Tennessee from 1907 to 1916. He wrote 'I'll Take You Home Again, Kathleen' for his wife.

Wharton, Thomas (1648–1714) was born to a titled, parliamentarian family in Buckinghamshire. He wrote 'Lilliburléro' in opposition to the pro-Catholic policies of James II in Ireland and later held public office in England under William III.

Wilson, Florence Mary (d. 1947) was born in Warrenpoint and died in Bangor. She is remembered chiefly as the author of 'The Man from God-Knows-Where.

Wolfe, Charles (1791–1823) was born in Blackhall, County Kildare, and educated in TCD. He became a curate in 1817 and in the same year his famous ode was published anonymously. He died of tuberculosis in Cork.

Yeats, William Butler (1865–1939) was born in Dublin but spent much of his boyhood with his mother's family, the Pollexfens, in Sligo and the rich folklore of the region had a significant influence on him. He won the Nobel Prize for Literature in 1923 and died in Roquebrune, in the south of France, where he had settled for the sake of his health.

'Zozimus': the nickname of the street-ballad-maker Michael Moran (1794–1846), who was born off Lower Clanbrassil Street in Dublin's Liberties. He went blind at two weeks and made his living by performing comic and topical ballads (his own and those of others), which he rapped rather than sang as he had no ear for music. He acquired his nickname from the frequent recitation of the poem 'St Mary of Egypt', about the conversion of a 5th-century harlot by Bishop Zozimus.

Index of First Lines

The beauty of the world hath made me sad, 195
The cat went here and there, 114
The Garden of Eden has vanished they say, 247
The night before Larry was stretched, 141
The night is gathering gloomily, the day is closing fast , 15
The pale moon was rising above the green mountain, 242
The savage loves his native shore, 69
The ship it sails in half an hour to cross the broad Atlantic, 80
The sons of the Prophet are brave men and bold, 156
The trees are in their autumn beauty, 113
The winter it is past, and the summer's come at last, 238
There our murdered brother lies, 13
There's a colleen fair as May, 208
There's a dear little plant that grows in our isle, 68
There's a sweet garden spot in our memory, 244
There's music in my heart all day, 74
Tim Finnegan lived in Walkin Street, 132
'Tis I go fiddling, fiddling, 194
To Rathlin's Isle I chanced to sail, 171
Trasna na dtonnta, 'dul siar 'dul siar, 266
Tráthnóinín beag déanach 's mo thréada agam á gcur ón síón, 262
Tráthnóinín déanach i gcéin cois leasa dom, 263
Up the airy mountain, 182
We are the music-makers, 185
We were sittin' on the wall upon a Sunday, 229
What's the news What's the news, O my bold Shelmalier, 45
When all besides a vigil keep, 31
When boyhood's fire was in my blood, 29
When Éire first rose from the dark-swelling flood, 66
When first I saw sweet Peggy, 239
When, on Ramillies' bloody field, 25
Where dips the rocky highland, 191
Where Foyle his swelling waters, 19
While going the road to sweet Athy, 203
While shepherds watched their flocks by night, 168
Who fears to speak of Ninety-eight, 34
Will you come the bower o'er the free boundless ocean, 64
You've heard o' Julius Caesar an' the great Napoleon, too, 160